RESILIENCE REIMAGINED

Navigating a World Transformed by Crisis

TL Bell

CONTENTS

Title Page

Introduction   1

Chapter I   8

Chapter II   16

Chapter III   23

Chapter IV   31

Chapter V   40

Chapter VI   50

Chapter VII   62

Chapter VIII   75

Chapter IX   87

Chapter X   99

Conclusion   111

Recommendations   113

About The Author   119

Books By This Author   121

INTRODUCTION

The concept of a world transformed by crisis envisions a global landscape profoundly altered by significant challenges, disruptions, or upheavals. Crises can take various forms, including pandemics, economic recessions, environmental disasters, geopolitical conflicts, and more. The transformative impact of such crises extends beyond immediate consequences, shaping the trajectory of societies, economies, and international relations. Here are key aspects to consider in understanding a world transformed by crisis:

1. Paradigm Shifts:
   Crises often trigger paradigm shifts in societal norms, values, and priorities.
   The ways individuals, communities, and nations perceive and approach challenges undergo fundamental changes.

2. Reevaluation of Systems:
   Existing systems, whether economic, political, or social, face scrutiny and reevaluation.
   Crises expose vulnerabilities and inefficiencies, prompting a reassessment of institutional structures.

3. Accelerated Innovation:
   Crises act as catalysts for accelerated innovation and technological advancements.
   Societal challenges drive the adoption of new technologies and solutions for crisis response.

4. Crisis Driven Adaptation:
   Adaptation becomes a necessity, leading to the development of resilience strategies at individual, community, and institutional levels.

The ability to adapt becomes a critical determinant of survival and success.

5. Global Interconnectedness:
Crises underscore the interconnected nature of the global community.
Collaborative approaches and international cooperation become essential for addressing shared challenges.

6. Social Solidarity:
Crises often evoke a sense of solidarity among individuals and communities.
Altruism, empathy, and a collective spirit emerge as people unite to overcome adversity.

7. Rethinking Priorities:
Societal priorities undergo a paradigm shift as communities reevaluate what matters most.
Issues such as health, environmental sustainability, and social justice may gain heightened importance.

8. Economic Restructuring:
Crises can lead to economic restructuring, impacting industries, job markets, and global trade.
New economic models may emerge as societies navigate recovery and growth.

9. Environmental Awareness:
Environmental crises contribute to an increased awareness of ecological issues.
Sustainable practices gain prominence as societies recognize the importance of protecting the planet.

10. Changes in Governance:
Crises may prompt changes in governance structures and political systems.
Calls for transparent, accountable, and inclusive governance become more pronounced.

11. Health Security Prioritization:
    Health crises elevate the importance of healthcare systems and public health measures.
    Investments in healthcare infrastructure and global health security gain significance.

12. Digital Transformation:
    Crises accelerate the digital transformation of societies.
    Remote work, online education, and digital communication become integral components of daily life.

13. Cultural Shifts:
    Cultural norms and behaviors undergo shifts in response to crises.
    New cultural narratives may emerge, reflecting resilience, adaptability, and a collective memory of overcoming challenges.

14. Global Reflection and Learning:
    Crises prompt reflection on past responses and lessons learned.
    The global community becomes more adept at anticipating and mitigating future crises.

15. Preparedness and Resilience Culture:
    Crises cultivate a culture of preparedness and resilience.
    Individuals, communities, and nations proactively invest in strategies to mitigate future risks.

A world transformed by crisis is characterized by its capacity to evolve, learn, and innovate in the face of challenges. While crises bring about disruptions, they also present opportunities for positive change, growth, and the emergence of more resilient, adaptable, and interconnected societies. The key lies in the collective response to crises, fostering a shared commitment to building a better and more sustainable world.

In the wake of profound and impactful crises, the world undergoes a transformative journey, reshaping its very fabric and presenting a landscape defined by challenges and opportunities previously unseen. The concept of a world transformed by crisis encapsulates the dynamic shifts in societal, economic, and geopolitical spheres, as well as the deep impact on individual lives. It is a narrative that goes beyond immediate survival needs, delving into the complexities and nuances of the aftermath —examining psychological trauma, societal restructuring, and the emergence of new challenges that demand innovative solutions. This transformative journey invites exploration into the resilience required to navigate this changed world and the potential for positive adaptation and growth. This is a comprehensive exploration of the multifaceted challenges and opportunities that arise in the aftermath of a crisis, offering readers insights and strategies for navigating a transformed world.

Beyond the urgency of immediate survival needs, a transformed world post-crisis introduces a host of unique challenges that demand attention and understanding. These challenges extend into various dimensions of human existence, presenting complexities that shape the new normal. Here are some key highlights:

Psychological Trauma:
The aftermath of a crisis leaves a lasting impact on mental health, with individuals and communities grappling with trauma and emotional distress.
Coping mechanisms and mental well being become critical aspects of post crisis recovery.

Social Disintegration:
Societal structures may experience breakdowns, leading to a fragmentation of communities and a sense of disconnection.
Rebuilding social cohesion becomes essential for fostering resilience and collective recovery.

Economic Inequality:

Crises often exacerbate existing economic disparities, widening the gap between privileged and vulnerable populations.

Addressing economic inequality becomes a pivotal challenge for sustainable recovery and societal stability.

Technological Dependency:

Increased reliance on technology may deepen digital divides, affecting access to information, education, and essential services.

Balancing technological advancements with equitable access becomes crucial for societal cohesion.

Biosecurity Concerns:

The focus on public health intensifies, leading to heightened awareness and concerns about biosecurity.

Striking a balance between health precautions and individual freedoms poses a challenge in the post crisis landscape.

Information Warfare:

The vulnerability to misinformation and information warfare challenges societal trust and decision making.

Safeguarding information integrity and promoting media literacy become critical imperatives.

Education Gaps:

Disruptions in education during crises may widen existing gaps, posing challenges in providing equitable learning opportunities.

Innovative solutions for remote learning and addressing educational disparities become paramount.

Urban Rural Dynamics:

Shifts in population distribution and urban rural dynamics may impact resource allocation and regional development.

Balancing the needs of urban and rural areas becomes a complex challenge for policymakers.

Human Rights Challenges:

Crisis responses may inadvertently pose challenges to human

rights, necessitating a careful balance between security measures and individual freedoms.

Upholding human rights principles becomes a crucial aspect of ethical governance.

Building Resilient Societies:

Long-term planning for resilient infrastructure and healthcare systems becomes imperative to withstand future shocks.

Environmental sustainability and community resilience take center stage in shaping a robust societal framework.

These challenges, extending beyond immediate survival, present a roadmap for navigating the complexities of a transformed world, requiring strategic and thoughtful responses to foster sustainable recovery and growth.

As we embark on a journey through the intricacies of a world transformed by crisis, it is essential to set the stage for an in-depth exploration of the challenges that extend far beyond the realm of immediate survival needs. The aftermath of crises introduces a complex tapestry of societal shifts, psychological struggles, and structural transformations that demand our attention and collective introspection.

In understanding the profound impact of psychological trauma, we delve into the human experience, recognizing the scars left on individual minds and the collective psyche. Societal disintegration poses questions about our ability to rebuild connections and foster resilience in the face of adversity. Economic inequality, exacerbated by crises, forces us to confront the disparities that threaten the very fabric of our social cohesion.

As we navigate the terrain of technological dependency and the pitfalls of information warfare, we confront the dual-edged sword of innovation that demands thoughtful regulation and equitable access. Biosecurity concerns compel us to rethink the delicate balance between health precautions and personal freedoms.

The widening gaps in education and the evolving urban-rural dynamics beckon us to reassess our priorities for a more inclusive and sustainable future.

Yet, amidst these challenges, lies the opportunity for transformation and growth. This exploration is not a mere cataloging of difficulties but an invitation to engage in dialogue and action. It is a call to consider innovative solutions, ethical frameworks, and strategic planning that can pave the way for a resilient, adaptive, and equitable society.

Throughout this journey, we will seek not only to understand the complexities of the post-crisis landscape but also to propose actionable solutions. The goal is not just to navigate these challenges but to emerge stronger, wiser, and more united. It is an exploration that transcends the immediate aftermath, envisioning a future where the lessons learned from crisis propel us towards a more sustainable and compassionate world. Join us as we embark on this intellectual expedition, where challenges become opportunities and solutions light the path to a reimagined resilience.

CHAPTER I

Aftermath Realities

In the aftermath of a profound crisis, the realities that unfold extend far beyond the immediate impact, shaping the very essence of individuals and societies. This chapter, titled "Aftermath Realities," delves into the complex landscape that emerges, marked by psychological trauma, societal transformations, and economic repercussions.

Psychological Trauma:
The chapter begins by exploring the profound psychological impact of crisis events. Individuals and communities grapple with trauma, grief, and emotional distress. Through personal narratives and expert insights, we uncover the long-lasting effects on mental health and the imperative of addressing psychological well being in the recovery process.

Societal Disintegration:
As societal structures experience disruptions, we examine the breakdown of social bonds and community ties. The narrative unfolds through the lens of those directly affected, illustrating the challenges of rebuilding social cohesion and fostering resilience in the face of a fractured societal landscape.

Economic Inequality:
The economic repercussions of a crisis often exacerbate existing disparities. This section investigates the widening gap between different socioeconomic strata, analyzing the root causes and consequences. Expert interviews and case studies provide a comprehensive view of the economic challenges faced by individuals and communities.

The exploration of "Aftermath Realities" sets the stage for understanding the multifaceted nature of the challenges post-crisis, laying the groundwork for subsequent chapters to delve into solutions and pathways towards recovery and renewal.

The psychological trauma experienced by individuals and a community in the aftermath of a crisis is profound and multifaceted. This trauma stems from the emotional and mental distress caused by exposure to distressing events, loss, uncertainty, and the disruption of normalcy. Let's explore the various dimensions of psychological trauma:

1. Immediate Impact:
   Individuals often face acute stress reactions during and immediately after a crisis, triggered by fear, shock, and survival instincts.
   Communities witness a collective sense of vulnerability and loss, leading to heighten emotional responses.

2. Grief and Loss:
   Grieving the loss of lives, property, and a sense of security is a pervasive experience.
   Individuals and communities grapple with the emotional toll of saying goodbye to loved ones and the familiar.

3. Post Traumatic Stress Disorder (PTSD):
   Some individuals may develop PTSD, characterized by intrusive memories, flashbacks, nightmares, and heightened arousal.
   The ongoing impact of trauma can interfere with daily functioning, relationships, and overall well-being.

4. Collective Trauma:
   Communities undergo a form of collective trauma, where shared experiences shape the group's identity and resilience.
   Shared grief and recovery efforts can contribute to a sense of community strength, but they also present unique challenges.

5. Survivor's Guilt:

Those who survive a crisis may experience guilt, questioning why they lived while others perished.

This emotional burden can lead to a profound sense of responsibility and a complex array of emotions.

6. Fear of Recurrence:

Anxiety and fear about the possibility of a recurrence of the crisis can persist long after the event.

Individuals may struggle with hypervigilance and heightened anxiety, impacting their ability to feel safe.

7. Loss of Trust and Safety:

The erosion of a sense of trust and safety is common, both at an individual and community level.

Rebuilding trust becomes a crucial component of the healing process.

8. Long-Term Mental Health Impacts:

Psychological trauma can contribute to long-term mental health challenges, such as depression, anxiety disorders, and substance abuse.

Access to mental health services becomes critical for recovery.

9. Coping Mechanisms and Resilience:

Individuals and communities develop coping mechanisms and resilience strategies to navigate the emotional challenges.

Support networks, counseling services, and community initiatives play a vital role in fostering resilience.

Understanding and addressing psychological trauma is a fundamental aspect of post crisis recovery. Mental health support, community initiatives, and societal empathy contribute to the healing process, enabling individuals and communities to rebuild their lives and move forward.

The breakdown of social structures in the aftermath of a crisis is a profound and complex phenomenon that reshapes the fabric of societies. This breakdown can manifest in various ways, impacting interpersonal relationships, community dynamics, and the functioning of institutions. Let's examine the breakdown of social structures and its far-reaching impact:

1. Disruption of Social Bonds:
Crisis events often disrupt the normal functioning of social networks and relationships.
Displacement, loss of communication channels, and the upheaval of daily life contribute to a breakdown in interpersonal connections.

2. Community Fragmentation:
The cohesion within communities may erode as individuals and families face unique challenges and priorities.
Divisions may emerge as communities grapple with resource scarcity, competing needs, and differing perspectives on recovery.

3. Erosion of Trust:
The breakdown of social structures can lead to a decline in trust among community members and between individuals and institutions.
Trust is essential for cooperation, collective decision making, and the successful implementation of recovery initiatives.

4. Challenges in Communication:
Disruptions in communication infrastructure and channels hinder the flow of information.
Miscommunication or the lack of reliable information often contributes to confusion and mistrust.

5. Impact on Vulnerable Populations:
Vulnerable populations, such as the elderly, children, and marginalized groups, may face increased isolation and challenges in accessing support.
Existing inequalities may be exacerbated, leading to further marginalization.

6. Strain on Social Services:

The demand for social services often surges in the aftermath of a crisis, placing strain on institutions and resources.

Overburdened social systems may struggle to meet the diverse needs of a population in distress.

7. Changes in Social Norms:

Crisis situations may prompt shifts in social norms as individuals and communities adapt to new circumstances.

Traditional roles and expectations may undergo transformation, sometimes challenging established cultural norms.

8. Increased Vulnerability to Exploitation:

The breakdown of social structures can create conditions where vulnerable individuals are more susceptible to exploitation and abuse.

Human rights violations may increase in the absence of protective social frameworks.

9. Challenges in Governance:

Institutions of governance may face disruptions, affecting their ability to provide stability and address societal needs.

The breakdown of governance structures can contribute to a sense of lawlessness and insecurity.

10. Rebuilding Social Cohesion:

Rebuilding social structures involves intentional efforts to restore trust, communication, and community ties.

Community led initiatives, support networks, and collaborative projects play a vital role in fostering resilience and recovery.

Understanding the impact of the breakdown of social structures is crucial for developing effective strategies to rebuild communities and strengthen social cohesion in the aftermath of a crisis. It requires a holistic approach that addresses the interconnectedness of social, cultural, and institutional dimensions.

The intensification of economic disparities in the aftermath of a crisis is a pervasive and complex phenomenon that often exacerbates existing inequalities within societies. Crises can disproportionately affect different socioeconomic groups, leading to increased disparities in income, wealth, and access to resources. Let's discuss the factors contributing to the intensification of economic disparities post crisis:

1. Job Loss and Unemployment:
Economic downturns associated with crises often result in widespread job losses and increased unemployment rates.
Vulnerable populations, including low income workers and those in precarious employment, are disproportionately affected.

2. Impact on Small Businesses:
Small businesses, which may lack the financial resilience of larger corporations, face higher risks of closure during and after crises.
This can result in the loss of livelihoods for entrepreneurs and employees, contributing to economic inequality.

3. Financial Market Volatility:
Financial markets may experience increased volatility post crisis, affecting investment portfolios and exacerbating wealth disparities.
Individuals with significant investments may recover more quickly than those without.

4. Housing Disparities:
The housing market can be severely impacted, leading to disparities in access to affordable housing.
Vulnerable populations may face eviction and homelessness, while others can leverage the crisis for real estate investments.

5. Access to Education:
Economic disparities in education are heightened, as access to quality education becomes more challenging for low-income

families.

Disruptions in schooling and remote learning can disproportionately impact students without necessary resources.

6. Healthcare Disparities:
The economic fallout from a crisis can exacerbate existing healthcare disparities.

Individuals with limited financial resources may face barriers to accessing quality healthcare, worsening health outcomes.

7. Government Response and Fiscal Policies:
The nature of government response and fiscal policies post crisis can either mitigate or intensify economic disparities.

Bailout and stimulus packages may benefit certain industries and wealthy individuals more than others.

8. Technological Divide:
The reliance on technology for remote work, education, and communication can widen the technological divide.

Individuals without access to digital resources may face barriers in participating in the digital economy.

9. Impact on Informal Economy:
Crises can disproportionately affect the informal economy, where workers often lack job security and social protections.

Those relying on informal employment may struggle to recover economically.

10. Resource Allocation and Recovery Programs:
The allocation of resources and design of recovery programs may favor certain sectors or demographics.

Inequitable distribution of resources can perpetuate economic disparities rather than addressing them.

Addressing the intensification of economic disparities post crisis requires a comprehensive approach that includes targeted policies, social safety nets, and efforts to promote inclusive economic recovery. Failure to address these disparities can lead to long-lasting consequences, hindering the overall resilience and well being of societies.

CHAPTER II

Faces of Displacement

The consequences of mass displacement and increased migration in the aftermath of a crisis are multifaceted, impacting both the displaced populations and the host communities. These consequences extend beyond immediate challenges and can have lasting effects on social, economic, and political dynamics. Let's investigate the key consequences:

1. Humanitarian Challenges:

Mass displacement often leads to humanitarian crises, with displaced populations facing immediate needs for shelter, food, clean water, and medical care.

Overcrowded refugee camps and strained humanitarian aid resources can exacerbate the challenges.

2. Strain on Host Communities:

Host communities may experience strain on resources and services, including healthcare, education, and infrastructure.

Competition for jobs and housing can create tensions between displaced populations and host communities.

3. Economic Impact:

Displaced individuals may face challenges integrating into the labor market, leading to economic hardships for both displaced and host populations.

Informal economies in host communities may be affected, contributing to economic disparities.

4. Social Integration Challenges:

Cultural differences and language barriers can pose challenges to the social integration of displaced individuals within host communities.

Social tensions may arise, impacting community cohesion and relationships.

5. Education Disruptions:

Displaced children often face disruptions in education, with challenges in accessing schools and adapting to new curricula.

Host communities may experience increased pressure on educational infrastructure.

6. Healthcare Strain:

The strain on healthcare systems in both displaced and host communities can lead to challenges in providing adequate medical care.

Infectious diseases may spread more easily in crowded living conditions.

7. Security Concerns:

Mass displacement can pose security concerns, with the potential for increased crime rates and social unrest.

Host communities may perceive displaced populations as a security risk, contributing to tensions.

8. Long-Term Displacement:

Prolonged displacement can lead to a protracted refugee situation, with implications for mental health, education, and economic prospects.

Host communities may face enduring challenges associated with providing sustained support.

9. Cultural Changes:

The influx of diverse cultures and backgrounds can contribute to cultural changes in both displaced and host communities.

This can be an enriching aspect but may also lead to resistance or challenges in cultural adaptation.

10. Political Implications:

Mass displacement can have political implications,

influencing domestic and international politics.

Policies related to asylum, immigration, and humanitarian aid may be shaped by the presence of displaced populations.

Navigating the consequences of mass displacement and increased migration requires a comprehensive and collaborative approach involving international organizations, governments, NGOs, and local communities. Efforts to address humanitarian needs, promote economic integration, and foster social cohesion are essential for minimizing negative impacts and building resilient communities.

Behind the statistics and geopolitical considerations, the human stories behind forced relocations and migrations reveal the profound impact on individuals and families. These stories reflect the resilience, challenges, and aspirations of people navigating the complex and often traumatic experience of displacement. Let's explore some common themes in these human stories:

1. Loss and Trauma:

Forced relocations often entail the loss of homes, possessions, and sometimes loved ones.

Families grapple with the trauma of sudden upheaval, leaving behind familiar environments and communities.

2. Search for Safety:

Many forced relocations are driven by a search for safety and escape from conflict, persecution, or environmental disasters.

Individuals and families embark on perilous journeys in pursuit of a more secure and stable life.

3. Resilience and Adaptation:

Displaced individuals demonstrate remarkable resilience and adaptability in the face of adversity.

Learning new languages, navigating unfamiliar cultures, and adapting to different social norms become integral parts of their journey.

4. Separation and Reunification:

Forced migrations often lead to the separation of families, with members scattered across different regions or countries.

Stories also emerge of the challenges and emotional reunification of families after periods of separation.

5. Educational Disruptions:

Displaced children and young adults often experience disruptions in their education.

Human stories highlight the determination to continue learning, overcoming barriers to access educational opportunities in new environments.

6. Cultural Preservation:

Migrants and refugees strive to preserve their cultural identity in the face of displacement.

Stories reveal efforts to maintain cultural practices, traditions, and languages as a way of connecting with one's roots.

7. Unpredictable Journeys:

Forced migrations often involve unpredictable and perilous journeys, whether by land, sea, or other means.

Human stories illuminate the challenges of navigating these journeys, including encounters with smugglers, dangerous conditions, and uncertainty.

8. Community Support and Solidarity:

Communities along migration routes and in host locations play a vital role in supporting displaced individuals.

Acts of kindness, solidarity, and support from local communities become central themes in these narratives.

9. Legal and Administrative Struggles:

Migrants and refugees frequently face legal and administrative challenges in seeking asylum or residency.

Human stories shed light on the complexities of navigating legal systems and bureaucratic hurdles.

10. Hopes for the Future:

Despite the hardships, human stories often reflect the enduring hopes for a better future.

Aspirations for stability, education, and opportunities for themselves and their families remain powerful motivators.

Exploring the human stories behind forced relocations and migrations humanizes the global issue of displacement. It underscores the need for empathy, understanding, and collaborative efforts to address the challenges faced by displaced individuals and create inclusive societies that embrace diversity and resilience.

The implications of forced relocations and migrations extend beyond the immediate challenges faced by displaced populations to impact the dynamics of host communities. Both groups experience a range of consequences that shape their social, economic, and cultural landscapes. Let's explore the implications for both displaced populations and host communities:

Implications for Displaced Populations:

1. Humanitarian Challenges:

Displaced populations often face immediate humanitarian challenges, including access to shelter, food, water, and healthcare.

2. Psychological Impact:

Forced relocations can result in significant psychological distress, trauma, and mental health challenges for individuals and families.

3. Educational Disruptions:

Displaced children and youth may experience disruptions in their education, leading to long-term consequences for their future opportunities.

4. Economic Struggles:

Finding employment in new environments can be challenging for displaced individuals, leading to economic hardships.

5. Legal and Administrative Challenges:
Navigating legal systems for asylum or residency can be complex, and displaced populations may face bureaucratic hurdles and uncertainties.

6. Cultural Adaptation:
The process of adapting to new cultures, languages, and social norms is a significant aspect of the displacement experience.

7. Health Risks:
Displaced populations may face health risks due to overcrowded living conditions, lack of access to sanitation, and strained healthcare systems.

8. Family Separation:
Forced migrations often result in family separations, leading to emotional distress and challenges in maintaining familial bonds.

9. Aspirations for Stability:
Despite the challenges, displaced populations often harbor hopes and aspirations for stability, security, and opportunities for themselves and their families.

Implications for Host Communities:

1. Strain on Resources:
Host communities may experience strain on resources, including healthcare, education, housing, and infrastructure.

2. Economic Impact:
The arrival of displaced populations can impact the local job market and economic dynamics, both positively and negatively.

3. Social and Cultural Changes:
The influx of diverse cultures and backgrounds can lead to social and cultural changes in host communities, fostering diversity but also presenting challenges.

4. Integration Challenges:

Host communities may face challenges in integrating displaced individuals, especially when it comes to language barriers and cultural differences.

5. Social Tensions:

Competition for jobs, resources, and services can lead to social tensions between displaced populations and host communities.

6. Solidarity and Compassion:

Acts of kindness, solidarity, and compassion from host communities can contribute positively to the integration of displaced populations.

7. Community Building:

The presence of displaced populations may prompt community building initiatives, fostering a sense of shared responsibility and support.

8. Economic Opportunities:

While there may be economic challenges, the presence of displaced populations can also create economic opportunities for local businesses and services.

9. Political Implications:

The arrival of displaced populations can have political implications, influencing local and national political discourse.

Understanding and addressing these implications require a holistic and collaborative approach that involves the active participation of governments, international organizations, local communities, and displaced populations themselves. Efforts to promote integration, social cohesion, and economic opportunities can contribute to positive outcomes for both displaced populations and host communities.

CHAPTER III

Unrest in Transition

The rise in civil and social unrest in the aftermath of a crisis is a complex and multifaceted phenomenon, influenced by a combination of economic, political, and social factors. Crises can amplify preexisting grievances and inequalities, leading to heightened tensions and expressions of discontent. Let's analyze the key factors contributing to the rise in civil and social unrest post crisis:

1. Economic Disparities:

Economic hardships resulting from the crisis, such as job losses, income inequality, and financial instability, can fuel frustration and discontent.

Perceptions of economic injustice may contribute to protests and social unrest as communities demand economic reforms.

2. Unemployment and Poverty:

High levels of unemployment and poverty following a crisis can create a sense of desperation and hopelessness, driving individuals and communities to protest for economic opportunities and social support.

3. Perceived Injustice and Corruption:

Perceived injustice, corruption, and a lack of transparency in crisis response and recovery efforts can erode public trust in institutions.

Citizens may take to the streets to demand accountability and reforms in governance.

4. Social Inequality:

Existing social inequalities can be exacerbated by the impact of a crisis, leading to heightened awareness and demands for social justice.

Movements addressing issues like racial or gender inequality may gain momentum.

5. Political Instability:

The upheaval caused by a crisis may create political instability, and disagreements over leadership and governance may result in protests and demonstrations.

6. Restrictions on Civil Liberties:

Imposition of emergency measures, restrictions on civil liberties, or perceived government overreach in crisis management can provoke public resistance and calls for the protection of rights.

7. Discontent with Crisis Response:

Dissatisfaction with the government's crisis response, whether due to perceived inefficiency, lack of transparency, or unequal distribution of aid, can contribute to social unrest.

8. Ethnic and Social Tensions:

Crisis situations may intensify existing ethnic or social tensions, leading to conflicts and unrest between different groups within a society.

9. Communication Breakdown:

A breakdown in communication between authorities and the public can foster mistrust and exacerbate tensions, contributing to social unrest.

10. Global and Local Solidarity Movements:

Global movements and solidarity efforts may influence local populations to mobilize for common causes, transcending national boundaries.

11. Access to Information and Technology:

Access to information and technology can empower individuals to organize and mobilize, contributing to the rapid spread of social movements.

12. Youth Mobilization:

Younger generations, often disproportionately affected by crises, may become catalysts for social movements seeking change and reform.

Understanding these factors is crucial for policymakers and authorities to address the root causes of unrest and implement measures that promote social cohesion, economic recovery, and transparent governance. Acknowledging and responding to the legitimate grievances of affected populations is key to fostering stability and resilience in the aftermath of a crisis.

Heightened tensions and potential conflicts in the aftermath of a crisis can arise from a combination of complex factors that exacerbate existing challenges and grievances. These factors, if unaddressed, may lead to social, political, or ethnic tensions that escalate into conflicts. Let's examine the key contributors to heightened tensions and potential conflicts post crisis:

1. Resource Scarcity:

Competition for limited resources, such as water, food, and shelter, can intensify tensions among communities, leading to conflicts over access and distribution.

2. Economic Disparities:

Widening economic disparities and unequal access to opportunities can create resentment and frustration, contributing to social and class based tensions.

3. Political Instability:

Instability in governance and leadership, especially during the aftermath of a crisis, can create power vacuums and political uncertainty, fueling tensions among competing factions.

4. Ethnic and Religious Differences:

Existing ethnic or religious differences may be exacerbated during a crisis, leading to increased identity based tensions and potential conflicts.

5. Displacement and Migration:
Mass displacement and increased migration can strain host communities and contribute to social tensions over resources, services, and cultural differences.

6. Nationalism and Patriotism:
Nationalistic sentiments may be heightened in the aftermath of a crisis, potentially leading to conflicts over national identity, borders, and geopolitical issues.

7. Political Ideologies:
Divergent political ideologies and conflicting visions for the post crisis recovery may lead to ideological tensions and disputes.

8. Competition for Aid and Assistance:
Competition for international aid and assistance can create tensions among groups or nations, especially if the distribution is perceived as unfair or unequal.

9. Security Concerns:
Heightened security concerns post crisis may lead to increased militarization and securitization, potentially escalating conflicts.

10. Environmental Stress:
Environmental degradation or resource depletion caused by the crisis can contribute to conflicts over land, water, or natural resources.

11. Humanitarian Crises:
Ongoing humanitarian crises resulting from the initial crisis can strain relief efforts and contribute to tensions over access to aid and assistance.

12. Disputed Territories:
Disputes over territorial boundaries, exacerbated by the crisis, can escalate into conflicts over control and ownership.

13. Historical Grievances:

Lingering historical grievances or unresolved conflicts may resurface in the aftermath of a crisis, reigniting tensions.

14. Weak Institutions:

Weak institutions, unable to effectively manage and resolve conflicts, can contribute to a lack of governance and perpetuate tensions.

15. External Influence:

External actors, such as neighboring countries or international organizations, may exert influence in a way that exacerbates tensions and conflicts.

Addressing these factors requires a comprehensive approach that includes conflict resolution mechanisms, inclusive governance, economic development, and initiatives promoting social cohesion. Early intervention, dialogue, and efforts to address the root causes of tensions are essential for preventing conflicts and fostering stability in post crisis environments.

Fostering stability and rebuilding trust in the aftermath of a crisis requires a comprehensive and multifaceted approach that addresses social, economic, and political dimensions. Here are strategies to promote stability and rebuild trust in post crisis environments:

1. Inclusive Governance:

Foster inclusive governance structures that involve diverse stakeholders in decision making processes.

Promote transparency, accountability, and responsiveness to the needs of the population.

2. Conflict Resolution Mechanisms:

Establish and strengthen conflict resolution mechanisms to address grievances and disputes.

Encourage dialogue and mediation to resolve conflicts peacefully.

3. Community Engagement and Participation:

Facilitate active participation of communities in the recovery and rebuilding process.

Involve local leaders, community organizations, and individuals in decision making and planning.

4. Reconciliation Programs:

Implement reconciliation programs that aim to heal divisions and build bridges between communities.

Foster dialogue and understanding among different ethnic, religious, or social groups.

5. Economic Recovery and Opportunities:

Implement targeted economic recovery programs to address unemployment and economic disparities.

Create job opportunities and support entrepreneurship to empower individuals and communities economically.

6. Investment in Education:

Prioritize investment in education to provide access to quality learning opportunities for all.

Education can play a crucial role in breaking the cycle of poverty and promoting social cohesion.

7. Social Cohesion Initiatives:

Launch social cohesion initiatives that bring together diverse communities for shared activities and events.

Promote cultural exchange programs to celebrate diversity and foster unity.

8. Community Based Infrastructure Projects:

Initiate community based infrastructure projects that address local needs and contribute to the overall development of the region.

Involve communities in the planning and implementation of such projects.

9. Trauma Informed Support:

Provide trauma informed support services, including mental

health resources and counseling, to address the psychological impact of the crisis.

Recognize and address the trauma experienced by individuals and communities.

10. Human Rights Protection:

Strengthen human rights protection mechanisms to ensure the rights and dignity of all individuals.

Uphold principles of justice and equality in post crisis governance.

11. Media Literacy and Information Integrity:

Promote media literacy programs to enhance critical thinking and discernment.

Combat misinformation and disinformation by ensuring the integrity of information channels.

12. International Cooperation and Aid:

Foster international cooperation and aid to support post crisis recovery efforts.

Collaborate with international organizations to leverage resources and expertise.

13. Restorative Justice Programs:

Consider restorative justice programs that focus on repairing harm, rebuilding relationships, and reintegrating individuals into the community.

Emphasize accountability and rehabilitation rather than punitive measures.

14. Youth Empowerment:

Empower and engage youth in community building initiatives, education, and decision making processes.

Recognize the potential of young people as agents of positive change.

15. Environmental Sustainability:

Integrate environmental sustainability practices into recovery efforts, promoting resilience against future crises.

Address environmental stressors and contribute to long-term stability.

These strategies should be tailored to the specific context of each post crisis situation, considering the unique challenges and opportunities present in the affected region. A collaborative and participatory approach involving communities, local authorities, civil society, and international partners is essential for sustainable stability and trust building.

CHAPTER IV

Global Shifts

In the aftermath of a crisis, international relations and global cooperation often undergo significant changes as nations respond to shared challenges, reassess priorities, and collaborate on recovery efforts. The nature of the crisis, its global impact, and the responses of individual countries may influence the dynamics of cooperation. Let's explore some key changes that may occur in international relations and global cooperation post crisis:

1. Increased Multilateral Cooperation:
   Crises that have global repercussions often lead to an increase in multilateral cooperation among nations.
   International organizations, such as the United Nations, may play a central role in coordinating joint responses and resource mobilization.

2. Humanitarian Alliances:
   Humanitarian crises can foster the formation of alliances focused on providing aid, relief, and support to affected regions.
   Countries may collaborate to share resources, expertise, and logistical support in humanitarian efforts.

3. Diplomatic Engagement:
   Crisis situations may prompt heightened diplomatic engagement as countries seek to navigate complex challenges and build consensus on recovery strategies.
   Diplomatic channels may be utilized for conflict resolution and peace building efforts.

4. Global Health Cooperation:
   Health related crises can lead to increased global health

cooperation, with countries collaborating on research, vaccine development, and healthcare infrastructure improvement.

Organizations like the World Health Organization (WHO) may play a central role in coordinating global health responses.

5. Economic Recovery Initiatives:

Economic crises may stimulate collaborative efforts to stabilize global markets, address economic inequalities, and promote sustainable recovery.

International financial institutions and economic alliances may work together to implement stimulus measures and financial support programs.

6. Environmental Collaboration:

Environmental crises may spur international collaboration on climate change mitigation, conservation efforts, and sustainable development.

Nations may reassess environmental policies and commit to shared goals for a more sustainable future.

7. Scientific and Technological Cooperation:

Crises that highlight the importance of scientific and technological advancements may lead to increased cooperation in research and innovation.

Countries may collaborate on technological solutions, data sharing, and capacity building.

8. Security and Conflict Prevention:

Post crisis, there may be an emphasis on international cooperation to address security challenges and prevent conflicts.

Collaborative efforts may focus on peace building, conflict resolution, and addressing the root causes of instability.

9. Digital Cooperation:

The digital realm may become an arena for increased international cooperation on cybersecurity, data governance, and the regulation of emerging technologies.

Countries may work together to establish norms and standards for responsible digital behavior.

10. Migration and Refugee Cooperation:
Crises leading to mass displacement may prompt countries to collaborate on refugee and migration policies.

International agreements and initiatives may be established to address the humanitarian aspects of displacement.

11. Trade and Economic Agreements:
Economic crises may prompt nations to reconsider trade policies and engage in discussions on reshaping global economic structures.

Bilateral and multilateral trade agreements may be revisited to promote economic recovery and resilience.

12. Global Solidarity Movements:
Civil society and grassroots movements may foster global solidarity, influencing governments and international organizations to prioritize shared values and human rights.

While crises can strain international relations, they also provide opportunities for strengthened collaboration, collective problem solving, and the reevaluation of global priorities. The extent and nature of changes in international relations depend on the nature of the crisis and the willingness of nations to work together for the common good.

Crises have a profound impact on global dynamics, reshaping the way nations interact, collaborate, and navigate shared challenges. The effects of crises extend beyond borders, influencing political, economic, social, and environmental dimensions of international relations. Here are keyways in which global dynamics are reshaped by crises:

1. Shift in Priorities:
Crises prompt a reevaluation of national and international priorities. Issues such as health security, climate change, and economic resilience may gain prominence in global agendas.

2. Increased Multilateralism:

Crises often lead to an increased emphasis on multilateralism, with nations recognizing the need for collaborative approaches to address global challenges.

International organizations, alliances, and forums become central to coordinating responses and sharing resources.

3. Global Solidarity:

Crises foster a sense of global solidarity as nations come together to support affected regions.

Humanitarian assistance, resource sharing, and collaborative efforts become integral to addressing the immediate and long-term impacts of crises.

4. Health Diplomacy:

Health crises, such as pandemics, elevate the importance of health diplomacy. Countries engage in collaborative efforts to share information, coordinate research, and ensure global vaccine distribution.

5. Technological Acceleration:

Crises accelerate the adoption and development of technology as nations seek innovative solutions for challenges in healthcare, communication, and economic recovery.

Increased reliance on digital platforms may reshape global communication and collaboration.

6. Reshaped Global Economy:

Economic crises lead to shifts in the global economic landscape, impacting trade, investment, and financial systems.

Nations may reassess economic policies, trade relationships, and global supply chains for increased resilience.

7. Environmental Focus:

Environmental crises heighten awareness of the interconnectedness of ecosystems and the importance of sustainable practices.

Global efforts to address climate change, biodiversity loss, and environmental degradation gain momentum.

8. Security Reassessments:

Security dynamics are reassessed as nations confront new threats and vulnerabilities arising from crises.

Collaborative efforts may focus on nontraditional security challenges, including public health, cybersecurity, and climate related security risks.

9. Social and Cultural Exchange:

Crises may influence social and cultural dynamics through changes in migration patterns, international travel restrictions, and shifts in cultural exchange.

Nations may reassess policies related to multiculturalism and diversity.

10. Redefined Diplomatic Relations:

Crises can prompt nations to reevaluate diplomatic relations based on shared interests and collaborative approaches.

Diplomatic efforts may prioritize conflict prevention, crisis response coordination, and peace building.

11. Increased Resilience Planning:

Nations recognize the importance of resilience planning in the face of crises, leading to a focus on preparedness, adaptive capacity, and risk reduction.

Collaborative frameworks for disaster risk reduction and management become central to global strategies.

12. Human Rights and Social Justice:

Crises underscore the importance of human rights and social justice in global governance.

International cooperation may be directed towards addressing inequalities, promoting inclusivity, and safeguarding human rights.

13. Information and Disinformation Challenges:

Crises highlight challenges related to information and disinformation, prompting discussions on information integrity, media literacy, and global communication norms.

14. Shifts in Soft Power:

The way nations exercise soft power may be influenced by their response to crises, shaping global perceptions of leadership, compassion, and effectiveness.

15. New Norms and Standards:

Crises contribute to the establishment of new norms and standards in various areas, from public health protocols to ethical considerations in technological advancements.

Understanding how global dynamics are reshaped by crises is crucial for adapting to the evolving international landscape, fostering collaboration, and building resilience against future challenges. The lessons learned from crises shape the trajectory of global governance and cooperation in significant ways.

The promotion of global resilience involves the collective efforts of nations and international organizations to enhance the capacity of societies, systems, and communities to withstand, adapt to, and recover from various challenges, including crises and disasters. Here's an overview of the key roles that nations and organizations play in fostering global resilience:

1. Early Warning and Preparedness:

Nations and organizations contribute to global resilience by investing in early warning systems for natural disasters, public health threats, and other crises.

Preparedness measures, including drills, training, and contingency planning, help communities respond effectively to emerging challenges.

2. Information Sharing and Collaboration:

Nations and organizations play a crucial role in sharing information, best practices, and lessons learned on a global scale.

Collaboration fosters the exchange of knowledge and expertise, enabling countries to benefit from the experiences of others in building resilience.

3. Capacity Building:
Support for capacity building at the national and local levels is essential for enhancing resilience.

Nations and organizations may provide technical assistance, training programs, and resources to strengthen the skills and capabilities of communities in various domains.

4. Investment in Infrastructure:
Nations contribute to global resilience by investing in resilient infrastructure that can withstand and recover from shocks.

Organizations may provide financial support and technical expertise for infrastructure projects that prioritize resilience.

5. Health Systems Strengthening:
Nations and international health organizations working together to strengthen health systems globally.

Investments in healthcare infrastructure, training of healthcare professionals, and the establishment of robust healthcare networks contribute to global resilience, particularly in the face of pandemics.

6. Climate Adaptation and Mitigation:
Addressing climate change is a critical aspect of promoting global resilience.

Nations collaborate on climate adaptation and mitigation strategies, aiming to reduce the impact of extreme weather events, protect ecosystems, and build climate resilient communities.

7. Disaster Risk Reduction (DRR):
Nations engage in disaster risk reduction efforts to minimize the impact of natural and manmade disasters.

Organizations support DRR initiatives by providing technical expertise, financial resources, and facilitating knowledge sharing platforms.

8. Humanitarian Assistance and Response:

Nations and international humanitarian organizations play a vital role in providing rapid and effective response to crises.

Coordination mechanisms, such as the United Nations' humanitarian clusters, facilitate collaborative efforts in delivering aid and assistance.

9. Education and Awareness:

Building resilience requires educating communities on risks, vulnerabilities, and adaptive strategies.

Nations and organizations contribute to global resilience by promoting awareness campaigns, educational programs, and community engagement initiatives.

10. Research and Innovation:

Investment in research and innovation is crucial for developing new technologies, methodologies, and solutions to enhance resilience.

Nations and organizations support research initiatives that contribute to a better understanding of vulnerabilities and effective resilience building measures.

11. Policy Advocacy and Governance:

Nations and organizations advocate for policies that prioritize resilience at local, national, and international levels.

Good governance practices, transparency, and accountability contribute to effective resilience building.

12. Financial Support and Risk Financing:

Financial support mechanisms, including risk financing and insurance, help countries and communities recover from crises.

Organizations collaborate to establish financial instruments that enhance the financial resilience of nations facing various risks.

13. Digital and Technological Solutions:

Nations and organizations leverage digital technologies for early warning, communication, and data analytics to enhance resilience.

Collaboration in the development and deployment of technology plays a crucial role in global resilience.

14. Cross Sectional Collaboration:

Promoting resilience requires collaboration across sectors, including government, private sector, civil society, and academia.

Nations and organizations facilitate partnerships that address the interconnected nature of resilience challenges.

15. Post crisis Recovery and Reconstruction:

Supporting nations in post crisis recovery and reconstruction efforts is a key role.

Organizations provide financial aid, technical support, and expertise to help communities rebuild in a resilient and sustainable manner.

In summary, the roles of nations and organizations in promoting global resilience are interconnected and require collaborative efforts. By working together, nations and international organizations can contribute to building a more resilient world that can effectively navigate and recover from various challenges and crises.

CHAPTER V

Technology's Dual Edge

The increased reliance on technology, especially during and after crises, has become a significant aspect of modern societies. However, this heightened dependence on technology also raises concerns about potential digital divides, where certain populations or communities may have unequal access to digital resources and opportunities. Let's investigate these aspects further:

Increased Reliance on Technology:

1. Telecommuting and Remote Work:
   The COVID19 pandemic accelerated the adoption of remote work, emphasizing the importance of technology for maintaining productivity.
   Virtual collaboration tools, video conferencing platforms, and cloud services have become essential for remote work.

2. Online Education:
   The education sector has witnessed a shift toward online learning platforms and digital resources.
   Virtual classrooms, elearning platforms, and digital textbooks are increasingly used for education delivery.

3. Digital Health Solutions:
   Health crises have led to the increased use of telehealth services, remote monitoring, and digital health platforms.
   Technology plays a crucial role in tracking and managing health data, contact tracing, and vaccine distribution.

4. EGovernment Services:

Governments are leveraging technology to provide online services to citizens, from digital identity systems to electronic document submission.

Egovernance initiatives aim to enhance efficiency and accessibility of public services.

5. Digital Communication:

Social media, messaging apps, and other digital communication tools have become primary channels for staying connected.

Information dissemination during crises often relies on digital communication platforms.

6. ECommerce and Online Transactions:

The ecommerce sector has experienced significant growth, with consumers increasingly relying on online platforms for shopping and transactions.

Digital payment systems and contactless transactions have gained prominence.

Potential Digital Divides:

1. Access to Technology:

Unequal access to technology devices (computers, smartphones, etc.) may create disparities in the ability to participate in digital activities.

Affordability and availability of highspeed internet can contribute to digital divides.

2. Digital Literacy:

Disparities in digital literacy skills may hinder some individuals or communities from fully utilizing digital resources.

Education and training programs are essential to bridge the digital skills gap.

3. Infrastructure Disparities:

Rural or underserved areas may lack the necessary infrastructure for reliable internet connectivity.

Infrastructure development is crucial to ensure equitable access to digital services.

4. Social and Economic Disparities:
Socioeconomic factors can contribute to digital divides, with lower income households facing challenges in accessing technology.
The cost of devices, internet subscriptions, and digital services may pose barriers.

5. Education Inequities:
Students without access to digital devices or a reliable internet connection may face challenges in participating in online learning.
Educational disparities may widen if there is unequal access to educational technology.

6. Healthcare Disparities:
Vulnerable populations may have limited access to digital health services, exacerbating existing healthcare disparities.
Telehealth effectiveness depends on factors such as internet access and digital literacy.

7. Geographic Divides:
Urban rural divides can contribute to discrepancies in technology access and digital opportunities.
Bridging geographic divides requires targeted initiatives to expand digital infrastructure.

8. Language and Cultural Barriers:
Language and cultural considerations can impact digital inclusivity, with certain populations facing challenges due to language barriers or cultural differences.
Multilingual and culturally sensitive digital solutions are essential for inclusivity.

9. Digital Accessibility:
Individuals with disabilities may encounter barriers in

accessing digital content and services.

Ensuring digital accessibility standards is crucial for inclusivity.

10. Privacy and Security Concerns:

Unequal access to digital security measures and concerns about data privacy may contribute to disparities in the willingness to engage in digital activities.

Building trust in digital platforms is essential for widespread adoption.

Addressing digital divides requires a comprehensive approach involving governments, private sector entities, nonprofit organizations, and the international community. Initiatives should focus on enhancing infrastructure, promoting digital literacy, and ensuring affordability to create a more inclusive and equitable digital landscape.

Technological advancements bring about numerous benefits, but they also give rise to ethical dilemmas as societies grapple with the ethical implications of new capabilities. Here are some key ethical dilemmas arising from technological advancements:

1. Privacy Concerns:

Advances in surveillance technologies, data collection, and artificial intelligence raise concerns about the erosion of privacy.

The ethical dilemma involves balancing the benefits of enhanced security and convenience with the right to individual privacy.

2. Algorithmic Bias and Fairness:

Machine learning algorithms can exhibit bias based on the data they are trained on, leading to unfair and discriminatory outcomes.

Ethical dilemmas arise in addressing and preventing algorithmic bias to ensure fair and equitable treatment for all individuals.

3. Autonomous Systems and Responsibility:

Autonomous technologies, such as selfdriving cars and drones, raise questions about accountability in the event of accidents or unintended consequences.

Determining responsibility and liability for actions performed by autonomous systems is a complex ethical challenge.

4. Social Media Influence and Manipulation:

Social media platforms can be used to spread misinformation, manipulate public opinion, and influence elections.

The ethical dilemma involves finding a balance between free expression and preventing the misuse of technology for manipulation.

5. Job Displacement and Automation:

The automation of jobs and tasks through technology raises concerns about job displacement and economic inequality.

The ethical dilemma involves addressing the social impact of automation and ensuring a just transition for affected workers.

6. Biometric Data and Surveillance:

The use of biometric data for identification and surveillance poses ethical concerns related to individual consent, security, and potential misuse.

Striking a balance between security measures and protecting individuals' rights to control their biometric information is a complex ethical challenge.

7. Genetic Editing and Bioethics:

Advances in genetic editing technologies, such as CRISPR, raise ethical questions about the potential for designer babies, genetic enhancements, and unintended consequences.

Ethical dilemmas involve determining the limits of genetic manipulation and ensuring responsible use of these technologies.

8. Cybersecurity and Hacking:

The increasing frequency of cyberattacks and hacking

incidents raises ethical questions about the responsible use of technology for malicious purposes.

Balancing the need for robust cybersecurity measures with the potential for surveillance and privacy infringement is a challenge.

9. Artificial Intelligence and Decision Making:

AI systems are increasingly involved in decision making processes, raising concerns about transparency, accountability, and the potential for biases.

Ethical dilemmas involve ensuring fairness, accountability, and human oversight in AI driven decision systems.

10. Environmental Impact of Technology:

The production and disposal of electronic devices contribute to environmental degradation and electronic waste.

Ethical dilemmas involve finding sustainable practices in technology development and addressing the environmental impact of technological advancements.

11. Addiction and Technology Dependence:

The design of addictive features in technology, such as social media platforms and mobile apps, raises concerns about technology dependence and its impact on mental health.

Balancing user engagement with responsible design that prioritizes well-being is an ethical challenge.

12. Dual Use Technologies:

Technologies developed for peaceful purposes can potentially be repurposed for harmful uses, leading to dual use ethical dilemmas.

Striking a balance between innovation and preventing the misuse of technologies for harm is a complex ethical consideration.

13. Digital Inequality:

Disparities in access to technology and digital resources contribute to digital inequality.

Ethical dilemmas involve addressing the social impact of

unequal access and ensuring that technological advancements benefit all segments of society.

14. Weaponization of Technology:
The development and use of technology for military purposes raise ethical concerns about the consequences of weaponized technologies.

Striking a balance between technological innovation and preventing harm through responsible use is a critical ethical dilemma.

15. Neurotechnology and Brain Computer Interfaces:
Advances in neurotechnology and brain computer interfaces raise ethical questions about cognitive enhancement, privacy of thought, and potential misuse.

Ethical dilemmas involve establishing ethical guidelines and safeguards to protect individuals from potential risks.

Addressing these ethical dilemmas requires interdisciplinary collaboration, involving technologists, ethicists, policymakers, and the public. Establishing ethical frameworks, regulations, and responsible practices is crucial to ensure that technological advancements align with societal values and principles. Ongoing ethical reflection and dialogue are essential to navigate the complex ethical landscape of technological innovation.

Harnessing technology for positive outcomes involves intentional and ethical use of technological advancements to address societal challenges, promote well-being, and contribute to positive social impact. Here are strategies for leveraging technology for positive outcomes:

1. Ethical Development and Design:
Prioritize ethical considerations in the development and design of technologies.

Implement ethical design principles that prioritize user well-being, inclusivity, and privacy.

2. Human Centered Design:

Adopt a human centered design approach that involves understanding and addressing the needs, preferences, and concerns of end-users.

Solicit user feedback throughout the development process to ensure technologies are user friendly and culturally sensitive.

3. Social Impact Assessment:

Conduct social impact assessments to evaluate the potential effects of technologies on communities and individuals.

Identify and mitigate any negative consequences, ensuring that technologies contribute positively to societal well-being.

4. Education and Digital Literacy:

Invest in education and digital literacy programs to empower individuals with the skills needed to navigate and harness technology.

Promote awareness of ethical considerations and responsible use of technology.

5. Inclusive Innovation:

Foster inclusive innovation by ensuring that diverse voices and perspectives are represented in the development and deployment of technologies.

Address digital divides and promote equal access to technology across different demographics.

6. Open Source and Collaboration:

Encourage open source development and collaboration among diverse stakeholders.

Open collaboration fosters transparency, innovation, and the collective effort to address global challenges.

7. Technology for Social Impact:

Channel technological advancements toward addressing social and environmental challenges.

Support projects and initiatives that leverage technology

for positive social impact, such as healthcare solutions, environmental monitoring, and education tools.

8. Digital Inclusion Initiatives:

Implement initiatives to bridge the digital divide and ensure that marginalized communities have equal access to technology.

Provide affordable and accessible technology solutions to underserved populations.

9. Civic Tech and Governance Innovation:

Explore civic tech solutions that enhance citizen engagement, transparency, and accountability in governance.

Leverage technology to improve public services, streamline processes, and foster participatory decision making.

10. Tech for Sustainable Development:

Align technological innovations with the principles of sustainable development.

Support technologies that contribute to environmental sustainability, resource efficiency, and climate resilience.

11. Responsible AI and Automation:

Embrace responsible AI practices, ensuring transparency, fairness, and accountability in algorithmic decision making.

Consider the social impact of automation and implement policies to mitigate job displacement.

12. Digital Health Solutions:

Develop and deploy digital health solutions that enhance healthcare accessibility, affordability, and efficiency.

Promote telehealth, remote patient monitoring, and health informatics for improved healthcare outcomes.

13. Technology for Education:

Harness technology to enhance educational opportunities, especially in remote or underserved areas.

Support elearning platforms, digital resources, and tools that facilitate personalized and inclusive education.

14. Blockchain for Transparency:

Explore the use of blockchain technology for enhancing transparency, traceability, and accountability in various sectors, including supply chains and financial transactions.

15. Digital Philanthropy and Social Entrepreneurship:

Encourage digital philanthropy and support social entrepreneurs leveraging technology for positive social change.

Invest in projects that address societal challenges through innovative, technology driven solutions.

16. Tech for Disaster Response and Resilience:

Leverage technology for effective disaster response, early warning systems, and community resilience.

Develop and implement technologies that aid in disaster preparedness, response coordination, and recovery efforts.

17. Tech Ethics and Governance:

Establish ethical guidelines and governance frameworks for the responsible development and deployment of technology.

Encourage industry standards that prioritize ethical considerations and accountability.

18. Cross Sector Collaboration:

Foster collaboration among government, private sector, academia, and civil society to jointly address societal challenges.

Create platforms for interdisciplinary collaboration to maximize the positive impact of technology.

By adopting these strategies, stakeholders can contribute to a technology driven future that prioritizes positive outcomes, ethical considerations, and societal well-being. Ongoing reflection, collaboration, and commitment to responsible technology use are essential for ensuring that technological advancements align with human values and contribute positively to global progress.

CHAPTER VI

Biosecurity Imperatives

Heightened awareness and focus on biosecurity measures have become increasingly important in the face of emerging infectious diseases, global pandemics, and the potential for bioterrorism threats. Biosecurity involves measures to prevent, control, and respond to biological threats, whether natural or intentional. Several factors contribute to the increased attention on biosecurity measures:

1. Pandemic Preparedness and Response:

The COVID19 pandemic has underscored the importance of global preparedness and response to infectious diseases.

Nations and organizations are prioritizing biosecurity measures to detect, control, and manage pandemics effectively.

2. Emerging Infectious Diseases:

The rise of new and reemerging infectious diseases, such as Ebola, Zika, and various strains of influenza, has highlighted the need for robust biosecurity measures.

Global surveillance and early detection are critical components of preventing the spread of emerging diseases.

3. Bioterrorism Threats:

The potential for intentional release of biological agents as an act of bioterrorism has led to increased focus on security measures.

Governments and security agencies work to enhance capabilities for preventing, detecting, and responding to bioterrorism threats.

4. Advancements in Biotechnology:

Advances in biotechnology, including gene editing and synthetic biology, have raised concerns about the dual use potential of certain technologies.

Increased awareness of these capabilities has prompted efforts to regulate and secure potentially dangerous biological research.

5. Globalization and Connectivity:

The interconnected nature of the global community facilitates the rapid spread of infectious diseases.

International collaboration on biosecurity measures is essential to address threats that transcend national borders.

6. One Health Approach:

The One Health approach recognizes the interconnectedness of human, animal, and environmental health.

Biosecurity measures encompass a broader perspective, considering the health of ecosystems and the interface between humans and animals.

7. International Health Regulations (IHR):

The World Health Organization's International Health Regulations provide a framework for global cooperation in preventing and responding to public health emergencies.

Nations are urged to enhance their capacities to meet IHR requirements, reinforcing biosecurity measures.

8. Research Ethics and Dual Use Concerns:

The scientific community is increasingly aware of ethical considerations related to research that may have dual use potential.

Guidelines and oversight mechanisms are implemented to balance scientific advancement with biosecurity concerns.

9. Capacity Building and Infrastructure:

Many nations are investing in building the capacity and infrastructure necessary for effective biosecurity measures.

This includes the establishment of surveillance systems, diagnostic capabilities, and response mechanisms.

10. Public Health and Security Nexus:

The intersection of public health and national security is evident in the emphasis on biosecurity.

Governments recognize that a resilient and secure nation requires a robust public health infrastructure.

11. Education and Training:

Education and training programs in biosecurity are being developed to enhance awareness and capabilities among professionals in the field.

The goal is to have a skilled workforce capable of responding to biological threats.

12. Risk Communication:

Effective risk communication is integral to biosecurity measures, ensuring that the public and relevant stakeholders are informed about potential threats and response actions.

Transparent communication builds trust and encourages compliance with preventive measures.

13. Supply Chain Security:

Ensuring the security of supply chains for biological materials, pharmaceuticals, and medical equipment is critical.

Efforts are made to prevent the unauthorized access or manipulation of biological resources.

14. Global Collaboration and Partnerships:

International collaboration and partnerships are central to addressing biosecurity challenges.

Initiatives like the Global Health Security Agenda (GHSA) foster collaboration in strengthening global health security capacities.

15. Ethical Guidelines in Research and Innovation:

Ethical guidelines are established to govern research and innovation in the life sciences.

Responsible conduct in research helps prevent the misuse of

scientific knowledge and technologies.

The heightened awareness and focus on biosecurity measures represent a proactive and collaborative approach to addressing biological threats. As technological, geopolitical, and environmental factors evolve, the global community continues to adapt and strengthen biosecurity frameworks to protect public health and ensure the security of nations.

Managing global health threats presents a complex and dynamic landscape with a range of challenges and opportunities. These threats, including pandemics, infectious diseases, and other public health emergencies, require coordinated efforts at local, national, and international levels. Here's an exploration of the challenges and opportunities in managing global health threats:

Challenges:

1. Rapid Spread of Infectious Diseases:
Challenge: Infectious diseases can spread rapidly across borders, facilitated by global travel and interconnectedness.
Implication: Containment becomes challenging, requiring swift and coordinated responses to prevent widespread outbreaks.

2. Unequal Access to Healthcare:
Challenge: Disparities in healthcare access and resources exist globally, leading to differential capacities to respond to health threats.
Implication: Vulnerable populations may face greater challenges in receiving timely and adequate healthcare during emergencies.

3. Health Infrastructure Gaps:
Challenge: Many regions, especially in low income countries, lack robust health infrastructure, including adequate healthcare facilities and trained personnel.
Implication: Building and sustaining effective response

mechanisms is hindered, leaving populations more vulnerable to health threats.

4. Global Governance and Coordination:
Challenge: Coordinating a global response requires effective governance structures, collaboration, and communication among nations.
Implication: Gaps in global governance may result in delayed responses, inadequate resource mobilization, and fragmented efforts.

5. Vaccine Distribution and Equity:
Challenge: Ensuring equitable access to vaccines during pandemics is a complex challenge, with issues of distribution, supply chains, and vaccine hesitancy.
Implication: Disparities in vaccine coverage can prolong the duration and impact of health threats.

6. Antimicrobial Resistance (AMR):
Challenge: The rise of antimicrobial resistance poses a threat to the effectiveness of existing treatments for infectious diseases.
Implication: Treating infections becomes more challenging, and new, effective treatments may be slow to develop.

7. Climate Change and Emerging Diseases:
Challenge: Climate change contributes to the spread of vector borne diseases and alters disease patterns.
Implication: Adapting public health strategies to changing disease dynamics and addressing climate related health risks is essential.

8. Misinformation and Infodemics:
Challenge: The rapid dissemination of misinformation during health crises can undermine public trust and hinder effective responses.
Implication: Combating misinformation requires proactive communication strategies and public health education.

9. Biological Threats and Bioterrorism:
Challenge: The potential for intentional release of biological agents poses a security risk.
Implication: Preparedness for bioterrorism requires advanced surveillance, response capabilities, and international cooperation.

10. Ethical Dilemmas in Public Health:
Challenge: Balancing public health measures with individual rights and ethical considerations is complex.
Implication: Contentious ethical issues may arise, such as privacy concerns, mandatory vaccinations, and resource allocation.

Opportunities:

1. Global Collaboration and Solidarity:
Opportunity: Strengthening global collaboration and solidarity is crucial for a coordinated response.
Benefit: Joint efforts enhance information sharing, resource allocation, and the development of common strategies.

2. Advancements in Vaccine Technology:
Opportunity: Advances in vaccine technology, such as mRNA vaccines, offer new possibilities for rapid vaccine development.
Benefit: Accelerated vaccine development can contribute to more effective responses to emerging health threats.

3. Digital Health Technologies:
Opportunity: Digital health technologies, including telehealth, contact tracing apps, and health informatics, enhance surveillance and response capabilities.
Benefit: Improved data analytics and communication tools aid in monitoring and controlling the spread of diseases.

4. Global Health Security Investments:
Opportunity: Increased investments in global health security infrastructure and preparedness measures.
Benefit: Strengthening health systems and building capacity

enhances readiness for future health threats.

5. One Health Approach:
   Opportunity: Adopting a One Health approach that considers the interconnectedness of human, animal, and environmental health.
   Benefit: Comprehensive strategies addressing the root causes of health threats and preventing spillover from animals to humans.

6. Research and Innovation:
   Opportunity: Ongoing research and innovation in the life sciences contribute to a better understanding of diseases and the development of new treatments.
   Benefit: Scientific advancements lead to improved diagnostics, treatments, and preventive measures.

7. Public Health Education and Awareness:
   Opportunity: Prioritizing public health education and awareness campaigns to promote preventive measures and reduce misinformation.
   Benefit: Informed and empowered communities are more likely to actively participate in health interventions.

8. International Health Regulations (IHR):
   Opportunity: Strengthening adherence to and implementation of the World Health Organization's International Health Regulations.
   Benefit: Consistent standards and cooperation facilitate a more coordinated global response to health threats.

9. Capacity Building and Training:
   Opportunity: Investing in capacity building and training programs for healthcare professionals and emergency responders.
   Benefit: Enhanced preparedness and response capabilities at the local, national, and international levels.

10. Ethical Governance and Decision Making:

Opportunity: Prioritizing ethical considerations in public health governance and decision making.

Benefit: Upholding ethical principles ensures a fair and equitable response to health threats while respecting individual rights.

11. Innovative Financing Mechanisms:

Opportunity: Exploring innovative financing mechanisms, such as public private partnerships and pandemic bonds.

Benefit: Adequate and timely funding supports effective response measures and strengthens health systems.

12. Community Engagement and Social Cohesion:

Opportunity: Fostering community engagement and building social cohesion to ensure widespread cooperation.

Benefit: Communities actively involved in health measures contribute to a more effective and sustainable response.

13. Preparedness Exercises and Simulations:

Opportunity: Conducting regular preparedness exercises and simulations to test response capabilities.

Benefit: Identifying strengths and weaknesses in response systems, enabling continuous improvement.

14. Health Diplomacy:

Opportunity: Strengthening health diplomacy to facilitate international cooperation and collaboration.

Benefit: Diplomatic efforts enhance information sharing, resource mobilization, and joint response strategies.

15. Global Surveillance Networks:

Opportunity: Developing and maintaining global surveillance networks for early detection of potential health threats.

Benefit: Timely identification allows for prompt responses and containment measures.

Effectively managing global health threats requires a multifaceted and collaborative approach that addresses challenges while capitalizing on opportunities for innovation, cooperation, and preparedness. The lessons learned from past experiences, combined with ongoing efforts, contribute to building a more resilient global health system capable of responding to the evolving landscape of health threats.

The intersection of health, security, and ethical considerations represents a complex and interrelated framework where public health imperatives, national and global security concerns, and ethical principles converge. This intersection is particularly evident during health emergencies, pandemics, and other public health crises. Here's an examination of how health, security, and ethical considerations intersect:

1. Public Health and National Security:

Health Perspective: Protecting public health is a fundamental goal, involving disease prevention, healthcare provision, and pandemic preparedness.

Security Perspective: Ensuring public health is recognized as a critical component of national security, as health crises can have profound economic, social, and geopolitical implications.

Ethical Considerations: Balancing the need for security measures with the protection of individual rights and privacy is an ethical challenge. Ethical considerations also extend to resource allocation and prioritizing vulnerable populations.

2. Health Emergencies and Global Security:

Health Perspective: Addressing global health threats requires international collaboration, information sharing, and resource mobilization to prevent and control the spread of diseases.

Security Perspective: Global health threats can transcend borders, impacting global stability and cooperation. Effective responses contribute to international security and stability.

Ethical Considerations: Ethical challenges include ensuring equitable access to resources, vaccines, and healthcare globally, as well as addressing power differentials in international collaborations.

3. Bioterrorism and Biosecurity:

Health Perspective: Preventing and responding to bioterrorism threats involves preparedness for intentional releases of biological agents and effective public health responses.

Security Perspective: Bioterrorism is a security concern, and measures to prevent, detect, and respond to intentional biological threats are integral to national and global security.

Ethical Considerations: Balancing security measures with individual rights, privacy, and the responsible conduct of research in the life sciences is an ethical imperative.

4. Privacy and Surveillance:

Health Perspective: Surveillance is crucial for early detection and control of infectious diseases. Contact tracing and data collection aid in public health responses.

Security Perspective: Surveillance can be a security tool to monitor and respond to health threats, including bioterrorism and emerging infectious diseases.

Ethical Considerations: Striking a balance between the need for surveillance and respecting individual privacy is an ethical challenge. Ensuring transparency, consent, and data protection are key ethical considerations.

5. Allocation of Scarce Resources:

Health Perspective: During health emergencies, there may be a need to allocate scarce resources, such as medical supplies, ventilators, and vaccines, to maximize public health outcomes.

Security Perspective: Ensuring the availability and distribution of essential resources is crucial for maintaining societal stability and security during crises.

Ethical Considerations: Ethical challenges arise in determining fair and just allocation mechanisms, addressing vulnerabilities, and avoiding discrimination in resource distribution.

6. Dual Use Technologies:

Health Perspective: Advances in biotechnology have dual use

potential, contributing to both health innovations and potential risks.

Security Perspective: Dual use technologies can be repurposed for malicious purposes, posing security threats that require governance and oversight.

Ethical Considerations: Responsible conduct in research, ethical oversight, and the prevention of misuse are central ethical considerations in the development and use of dual use technologies.

7. International Health Regulations (IHR):

Health Perspective: The World Health Organization's International Health Regulations provide a framework for global cooperation in preventing, detecting, and responding to public health emergencies.

Security Perspective: Adherence to IHR is crucial for global security, ensuring a coordinated and transparent response to health threats.

Ethical Considerations: Ethical considerations include the fair and equitable implementation of IHR, avoiding stigmatization, and respecting national sovereignty.

8. Health Diplomacy:

Health Perspective: Diplomacy in health involves international cooperation, collaboration, and the exchange of knowledge and resources to address health challenges.

Security Perspective: Health diplomacy contributes to building international trust, stability, and security by addressing shared health concerns.

Ethical Considerations: Ethical considerations in health diplomacy include transparency, equity, and ensuring that collaborations prioritize the well-being of populations.

9. Ethical Dilemmas in Pandemic Response:

Health Perspective: Pandemic responses involve public health measures, vaccination campaigns, and healthcare delivery to mitigate the impact of the disease.

Security Perspective: Maintaining societal order and stability during a pandemic is a security consideration that aligns with public health goals.

Ethical Considerations: Ethical dilemmas include balancing public health measures with individual rights, addressing social determinants of health, and ensuring fair access to healthcare.

10. Health as a Human Right:

Health Perspective: Access to healthcare is considered a fundamental human right, emphasizing the importance of equitable health systems.

Security Perspective: Ensuring access to healthcare contributes to societal stability and security by addressing underlying health disparities.

Ethical Considerations: Ethical imperatives include advocating for health equity, addressing social determinants of health, and respecting the right to health.

The intersection of health, security, and ethical considerations requires a nuanced and multidisciplinary approach. Ethical principles, including transparency, equity, respect for autonomy, and justice, must guide decision making to ensure that responses to health threats are effective, just, and respectful of individual and collective rights. Achieving a balance between health and security imperatives while upholding ethical principles is crucial for a comprehensive and sustainable approach to global health challenges.

CHAPTER VII

InfoWars and Misinformation

The vulnerability to misinformation and information warfare has become a significant concern in the modern information age, with implications for individual beliefs, societal trust, and even geopolitical stability. Analyzing the factors contributing to this vulnerability and the potential consequences is crucial for developing strategies to address these challenges:

Factors Contributing to Vulnerability:

1. Digitalization and Social Media:
   Challenge: The widespread use of digital platforms and social media enables the rapid dissemination of information, both accurate and misleading.
   Impact: Misinformation can spread quickly, reaching large audiences and contributing to the vulnerability of individuals to false narratives.

2. Confirmation Bias and Filter Bubbles:
   Challenge: Individuals tend to seek information that aligns with their existing beliefs, creating filter bubbles and reinforcing confirmation bias.
   Impact: This bias can lead to the selective consumption of information, making individuals more susceptible to misinformation that aligns with their preconceptions.

3. Cognitive Biases and Heuristics:
   Challenge: Cognitive biases, such as availability heuristic and anchoring, influence how individuals process and interpret information.
   Impact: These biases can lead to quick, emotionally driven

judgments that may be more susceptible to misinformation.

4. Lack of Media Literacy:
Challenge: Insufficient media literacy skills among the public make it difficult for individuals to critically evaluate information sources.
Impact: Without the ability to discern credible sources from misinformation, individuals are more susceptible to believing and sharing false information.

5. Polarization and Echo Chambers:
Challenge: Societal polarization contributes to the creation of echo chambers, where individuals are exposed to a limited range of perspectives.
Impact: Echo chambers reinforce existing beliefs, making individuals less open to diverse viewpoints and more vulnerable to manipulation.

6. Algorithmic Amplification:
Challenge: Algorithms on social media platforms often prioritize content that generates engagement, leading to the amplification of sensational or misleading information.
Impact: Misinformation can receive disproportionate visibility, further contributing to its spread and influence.

7. Disinformation Campaigns:
Challenge: State and nonstate actors may engage in deliberate disinformation campaigns to manipulate public opinion.
Impact: Coordinated efforts to spread false narratives can exploit existing vulnerabilities and amplify the impact of misinformation.

8. Psychological Manipulation Techniques:
Challenge: Techniques such as emotional appeals, fear inducing content, and conspiracy theories can be employed to manipulate individuals psychologically.
Impact: Emotional manipulation can override rational judgment, increasing vulnerability to misinformation.

9. Speed of Information Transmission:
   Challenge: Information spreads rapidly online, often outpacing fact checking and verification processes.
   Impact: False information can become widely accepted before corrections or clarifications are disseminated, leading to sustained belief in misinformation.

Potential Consequences:

1. Erosion of Trust:
   Consequence: Proliferation of misinformation erodes trust in traditional media, institutions, and even democratic processes.
   Impact: Diminished trust can undermine social cohesion and the functioning of democratic societies.

2. Manipulation of Public Opinion:
   Consequence: Deliberate disinformation campaigns can manipulate public opinion, influencing elections, policy debates, and social attitudes.
   Impact: Strategic misinformation can shape narratives, potentially leading to decisions that do not align with the public interest.

3. Social Division and Polarization:
   Consequence: Misinformation can contribute to social division and polarization by reinforcing existing beliefs and creating adversarial dynamics.
   Impact: Polarization can hinder constructive dialogue and compromise, making it challenging to address societal challenges effectively.

4. Undermining Public Health:
   Consequence: Misinformation related to health issues, especially during public health crises, can undermine efforts to control the spread of diseases and vaccination campaigns.
   Impact: Reduced public adherence to health guidelines and vaccination can contribute to increased health risks.

5. Security Threats and Manipulation:

Consequence: Information warfare, including cyberattacks and influence operations, can pose security threats to nations and organizations.

Impact: Manipulation of information can be used to sow discord, exploit vulnerabilities, and achieve geopolitical objectives.

6. Economic Disruptions:

Consequence: Misinformation can contribute to economic disruptions by influencing investor confidence, market behavior, and consumer decision making.

Impact: Economic consequences may result from widespread belief in false narratives affecting markets or industries.

Strategies to Address Vulnerability:

1. Media Literacy Programs:

Strategy: Implement comprehensive media literacy programs to enhance critical thinking skills and empower individuals to evaluate information sources.

2. Transparency in Algorithms:

Strategy: Promote transparencies in algorithms used by social media platforms, ensuring users understand how content is prioritized and presented.

3. Fact Checking and Verification:

Strategy: Strengthen fact checking mechanisms to quickly identify and correct misinformation, providing accurate information to the public.

4. Collaboration Among Platforms:

Strategy: Encourage collaboration among social media platforms, technology companies, and fact checking organizations to share information and combat misinformation collectively.

5. Promotion of Diverse Perspectives:

Strategy: Promote platforms that facilitate exposure to diverse perspectives, reducing the impact of filter bubbles and echo chambers. Using common sense and reasoned logic
so as not to pervert morality.

6. Regulation and Accountability:

Strategy: Implement regulations to hold platforms accountable for the dissemination of misinformation, ensuring they take proactive measures to address the issue. An acceptable standardized set of criteria must be developed and used exclusively as the final authority.

7. Public Awareness Campaigns:

Strategy: Conduct public awareness campaigns on the risks of misinformation, emphasizing the importance of verifying information before sharing. Develop systems where the public can easily discern truth from deception.

8. International Cooperation:

Strategy: Foster international cooperation to address cross border disinformation campaigns and share best practices in countering misinformation.

9. Ethical Journalism Standards:

Strategy: Encourage adherence to ethical journalism standards, emphasizing accuracy, fairness, and responsible reporting in the media.

10. Digital Literacy in Education:

Strategy: Integrate digital literacy education into school curricula to equip students with the skills needed to critically evaluate online information. Teaching analytical thinking skills and reasoned logic are imperative regardless of platform.

Addressing the vulnerability to misinformation and information warfare requires a multifaceted and collaborative approach involving individuals, governments, technology companies, and civil society. By implementing comprehensive strategies, society can work toward mitigating the impact of misinformation and fostering a more informed and resilient public. Parents teaching children to discern truth and why truth is misrepresented is of utmost importance.

The impact of misinformation on societal trust and decision making is profound and multifaceted. Misinformation, defined as the dissemination of false or misleading information, has the potential to erode trust in institutions, undermine the democratic process, and shape individuals' beliefs and behaviors. Here's an exploration of the various ways misinformation influences societal trust and decision-making:

1. Erosion of Trust in Institutions:

Impact: Misinformation can lead to a loss of trust in traditionally trusted institutions such as government, media, and academic institutions.

Mechanism: When institutions are perceived as unreliable or complicit in spreading misinformation, public trust diminishes weakening the social fabric.

2. Polarization and Social Division:

Impact: Misinformation contributes to polarization by reinforcing preexisting beliefs and creating adversarial dynamics.

Mechanism: Individuals exposed to misinformation that aligns with their views may become more entrenched in their positions, leading to increased social division.

3. Undermining Public Confidence:

Impact: Misinformation can undermine public confidence in public health measures, scientific findings, and policy decisions.

Mechanism: If false information contradicts expert advice or official guidance, individuals may question the legitimacy of measures, leading to noncompliance.

4. Influence on Decision Making:

Impact: Decision making at individual and societal levels can be influenced by false or misleading information.

Mechanism: Belief in misinformation may lead individuals to make decisions that are not based on accurate information, impacting personal choices and behaviors.

5. Implications for Democratic Processes:

Impact: Misinformation poses a threat to democratic processes by shaping public opinion, influencing elections, and undermining the integrity of information.

Mechanism: Dissemination of false narratives, especially during election campaigns, can influence voters and manipulate the democratic decision making process.

6. Health and Safety Risks:

Impact: Misinformation related to health issues, such as false claims about treatments or vaccines, can pose significant health and safety risks.

Mechanism: Unfounded health information can lead individuals to make decisions that jeopardize their well-being, contributing to public health challenges.

7. Economic Consequences:

Impact: Misinformation can have economic consequences by influencing market behavior, investor confidence, and consumer decision making.

Mechanism: False information about economic indicators or industries may lead to market fluctuations and economic disruptions.

8. Erosion of Media Credibility:

Impact: Misinformation contributes to a loss of credibility for media outlets, particularly if they are perceived as platforms for spreading false information.

Mechanism: Individuals may question the reliability of news sources, contributing to a broader decline in media trust.

9. Amplification of Fear and Anxiety:

Impact: Misinformation can amplify fear, anxiety, and panic, especially during crises or emergencies.

Mechanism: False narratives that exaggerate threats or spread unfounded rumors contribute to heightened emotions and irrational decision making.

10. Social Influence and Behavioral Change:

Impact: Misinformation can influence social norms and behavior, leading to collective actions or protests based on false premises.

Mechanism: Belief in misinformation may motivate individuals to participate in collective actions that align with the false narratives they have encountered.

11. Impairment of Critical Thinking:

Impact: Misinformation impairs critical thinking skills by presenting distorted or fabricated information as facts.

Mechanism: Individuals exposed to misinformation may struggle to discern credible information, hindering their ability to make informed decisions.

12. Interference with Public Discourse:

Impact: Misinformation can distort public discourse by introducing false narratives and distracting from evidence based discussions.

Mechanism: Debates and discussions may be shaped by false premises, leading to less informed and constructive conversations.

13. Difficulty in Correcting Misinformation:

Impact: Once misinformation takes hold, it can be challenging to correct, leading to persistent false beliefs.

Mechanism: Cognitive biases may contribute to the "continued influence effect," where individuals retain misinformation even after corrections are provided.

14. Trust in Online Platforms:

Impact: Misinformation on online platforms can impact trust in the platforms themselves.

Mechanism: Individuals may question the credibility and reliability of online platforms that are perceived as enabling the spread of false information.

15. Diminished Trust in Expertise:

Impact: Misinformation can contribute to skepticism and diminished trust in expert opinions, scientific consensus, and authoritative voices.

Mechanism: Individuals exposed to conflicting information may question the expertise of professionals, contributing to broader erosion of trust in knowledge authorities.

Addressing the impact of misinformation on societal trust and decision making requires a comprehensive approach that includes media literacy education, fact checking initiatives, transparent communication from institutions, and regulatory measures to hold purveyors of misinformation accountable. By fostering a more informed and critical public, societies can mitigate the negative consequences of misinformation and strengthen the foundations of trust and evidence based decision-making.

Promoting information resilience involves empowering individuals and communities to critically evaluate and navigate the information landscape, particularly in the face of misinformation and disinformation. Here are strategies to enhance information resilience:

1. Media Literacy Programs:

Objective: Build critical thinking skills and the ability to assess the credibility of information sources.

Implementation: Integrate media literacy education into school curricula and offer public awareness campaigns emphasizing critical evaluation.

2. Digital Literacy Education:

Objective: Equip individuals with skills to navigate digital platforms, discern credible sources, and identify potential pitfalls.

Implementation: Provide training programs and workshops

on digital literacy, covering topics such as online fact checking, source verification, and recognizing misinformation.

With the understanding the even fact checkers can and are manipulated, implying even more detailed research to confirm facts.

3. Critical Evaluation of Sources:

Objective: Encourage individuals to critically evaluate information sources and distinguish between reliable and unreliable content.

Implementation: Promote awareness of trustworthy news outlets, fact checking organizations, and tools for assessing the credibility of websites. Too, expose to the public those not reliable and those fostering disinformation.

4. Fact checking Initiatives:

Objective: Establish and support fact checking organizations to verify and debunk false information.

Implementation: Encourage the use of fact checking websites and apps, and promote fact checking in media reporting. With the caveat that universally accepted fact checking criteria is utilized to verify without distortion any claims of misinformation. The system must be universal and provably trustworthy. Anything less is useless and adds to the problem.

5. Transparent Algorithms:

Objective: Advocate for transparency in algorithms used by online platforms to enhance awareness of content prioritization.

Implementation: Promote policies that require disclosure of algorithmic decision making processes and mechanisms used by platforms to combat misinformation.

6. Community Engagement:

Objective: Foster community discussions and collaboration to share information, correct misinformation, and build a sense of collective responsibility.

Implementation: Organize community forums, workshops,

and events to discuss information resilience, involving local leaders, parents, educators, and media professionals.

7. Cross Generational Dialogue:

Objective: Facilitate intergenerational discussions on information consumption habits, digital literacy, and critical thinking.

Implementation: Encourage open conversations between younger and older generations to share insights, experiences, and strategies for navigating the information landscape.

8. Psychological Resilience Training:

Objective: Enhance individuals' ability to withstand psychological manipulation and emotional appeals in misinformation.

Implementation: Integrate psychological resilience training into educational programs and mental health initiatives.

9. Inclusive Information Access:

Objective: Ensure equitable access to diverse and reliable information sources for all communities, with standards of morality being the underlying bedrock to insure a successful and prosperous society.

Implementation: Address digital divides, promote multilingual information access, and support initiatives that provide information to underserved populations.

10. Government and Institutional Accountability:

Objective: Hold governments, institutions, and media organizations accountable for transparent and ethical information practices.

Implementation: Advocate for and support policies that promote transparency, ethical journalism standards, and accountability for spreading misinformation, provided an honest provable trustworthy system is in place to discern truth from deceit.

11. International Collaboration:

Objective: Foster collaboration between countries to address cross border misinformation challenges.

Implementation: Establish international partnerships for information sharing, joint research, and coordinated responses to global misinformation threats.

12. User Generated Content Guidelines:

Objective: Encourage responsible content creation and sharing on social media platforms.

Implementation: Advocate for clear guidelines on user generated content platforms, including measures to identify and address misinformation.

13. Responsible Social Media Use:

Objective: Promote responsible social media behavior and encourage users to critically evaluate and fact check information before sharing. Caveat, fact checker must be a reliable system with universal proven criteria used to discern truth from deceit.

Implementation: Develop public awareness campaigns on responsible social media use and the potential impact of sharing misinformation.

14. Regular Information Audits:

Objective: Conduct regular audits of information sources and platforms to assess their accuracy and reliability. Who is to conduct the audit and what is the method used, become prime considerations that must be address and acceptable to the masses.

Implementation: Establish independent bodies or initiatives that periodically evaluate the credibility of information disseminated by various sources.

15. Adaptive Education and Training:

Objective: Ensure that education and training programs continually adapt to evolving information landscapes.

Implementation: Regularly update educational materials, training curricula, and awareness campaigns to address emerging challenges and trends in misinformation.

By implementing these strategies, stakeholders can contribute to building information resilience at individual, community, and societal levels. The goal is to empower individuals to navigate the information landscape critically, discern reliable sources, and contribute to a more resilient and informed society.

CHAPTER VIII

Education in Flux

Widening educational disparities and challenges in access are critical issues that have significant implications for social equity, economic development, and overall well-being. Examining these disparities involves understanding the factors contributing to unequal access to education and the consequences for individuals and societies. Here's an analysis of the widening educational disparities and challenges in access:

Factors Contributing to Widening Educational Disparities:

1. Economic Inequality:

   Challenge: Economic disparities contribute to unequal access to quality education.

   Mechanism: Affluent families can afford private schooling, tutoring, and resources, while lower income families may face financial barriers to quality education. Can the money/education link be severed?

2. Geographic Disparities:

   Challenge: Unequal distribution of educational resources between urban and rural areas.

   Mechanism: Urban centers often have better funded schools, qualified teachers, and educational infrastructure, while rural areas may face resource shortages. Can all educational institutions be resources equally?

3. Digital Divide:

   Challenge: Disparities in access to digital devices and the internet.

   Mechanism: The shift to online learning during the COVID19

pandemic highlighted the digital divide, with students lacking access to technology facing challenges in remote education.

4. Gender Disparities:
   Challenge: Gender based inequalities in access to education.
   Mechanism: Cultural norms, early marriage, and discrimination may limit educational opportunities for girls, particularly in certain regions.

5. Ethnic and Racial Disparities:
   Challenge: Unequal educational opportunities based on ethnicity or race.
   Mechanism: Discrimination, systemic bias, and historical inequalities contribute to disparities in educational outcomes. Discrimination has become more political than actual in practice.

6. Disabilities and Special Educational Needs:
   Challenge: Limited access for individuals with disabilities.
   Mechanism: Inadequate infrastructure, lack of specialized teachers, and social stigmas may hinder access to inclusive education for students with disabilities.

7. Language Barriers:
   Challenge: Limited access for individuals facing language barriers.
   Mechanism: Students from linguistic minority groups may face challenges in accessing education in a language they are not proficient in.

8. Conflict and Displacement:
   Challenge: Disruptions to education due to conflict, displacement, or humanitarian crises.
   Mechanism: Wars and crises can result in the destruction of educational infrastructure, displacement of students, and interruptions to regular schooling.

9. Quality of Education:
   Challenge: Disparities in the quality of education provided.

Mechanism: Schools in marginalized communities may lack qualified teachers, updated curricula, and essential resources, affecting the overall quality of education.

Consequences of Widening Educational Disparities:

1. Persistent Poverty:
Consequence: Limited educational opportunities contribute to a cycle of poverty.
Impact: Without access to quality education, individuals may face challenges in securing well paying jobs, perpetuating intergenerational poverty.

2. Reduced Economic Mobility:
Consequence: Educational disparities hinder economic mobility.
Impact: Limited access to higher education and vocational training can restrict individuals from advancing economically and reaching their full potential.

3. Social Inequality:
Consequence: Education gaps contribute to broader social inequalities.
Impact: Unequal educational opportunities reinforce social divisions, hindering the development of inclusive and cohesive societies.

4. Diminished Innovation and Productivity:
Consequence: Unequal access to education hampers innovation and productivity.
Impact: Societies miss out on the potential contributions of individuals who lack access to quality education, limiting overall economic and social progress.

5. Health Disparities:
Consequence: Limited education is linked to health disparities.
Impact: Individuals with lower educational attainment may face challenges in accessing healthcare, leading to health

inequalities.

6. Political Participation Gaps:

Consequence: Educational disparities can contribute to unequal political participation.

Impact: Individuals with limited education may face barriers in engaging politically, potentially leading to disenfranchisement and unequal representation.

7. Increased Social Tensions:

Consequence: Educational disparities can exacerbate social tensions.

Impact: Inequitable access to education may lead to social unrest and dissatisfaction, particularly if certain groups perceive systemic biases in educational opportunities.

Strategies to Address Widening Educational Disparities:

1. Equitable Funding:

Strategy: Ensure equitable distribution of funding to schools, addressing resource disparities.

2. Digital Inclusion:

Strategy: Bridge the digital divide by providing technology and internet access to all students, particularly in underserved areas.

3. Gender Equity Initiatives:

Strategy: Implement policies and programs to promote gender equity in education, addressing cultural and societal barriers.

4. AntiDiscrimination Measures:

Strategy: Implement antidiscrimination measures to address ethnic, racial, and linguistic disparities in education.

5. Inclusive Education Practices:

Strategy: Promote inclusive education practices that cater to students with diverse learning needs, including those with disabilities.

6. Conflict Sensitive Education:

Strategy: Develop and implement conflict sensitive education approaches to ensure continued learning in crisis affected regions.

7. Language Access Programs:
Strategy: Implement language access programs to address language barriers and ensure linguistic diversity in education.

8. Quality Improvement Initiatives:
Strategy: Invest in programs to enhance the quality of education, including teacher training, curriculum development, and infrastructure improvement.

9. Community Engagement:
Strategy: Engage communities in educational decision making processes to ensure that local needs and concerns are considered.

10. Affirmative Action Policies:
Strategy: Implement affirmative action policies to address historical and systemic inequalities, particularly in higher education. Caveat, only merit-based considerations are ethical and sustainable, otherwise setup for failure is inevitable. Discrimination against the capable and prepared will result in disaster.

11. International Cooperation:
Strategy: Foster international cooperation to address global educational disparities, sharing best practices and resources.

12. Early Childhood Education:
Strategy: Invest in early childhood education to ensure a strong foundation for future learning and reduces disparities from the early stages.

13. Mental Health Support:
Strategy: Provide mental health support services within educational settings to address emotional and psychological challenges faced by students.

14. Flexible Learning Models:
   Strategy: Implement flexible learning models, including online and blended learning, to cater to diverse educational needs.

15. Advocacy and Policy Reform:
   Strategy: Advocate for policy reforms that prioritize educational equity, ensuring those systemic issues are addressed at the policy level.

Addressing widening educational disparities requires a comprehensive and coordinated effort involving parents, governments, communities, international organizations, and other stakeholders. By implementing these strategies, societies can work towards creating a more equitable and inclusive education system that benefits individuals and fosters sustainable development.

Innovative approaches are crucial to addressing education gaps post crisis and ensuring that all students have access to quality learning opportunities. Here are several innovative strategies and approaches to bridge education gaps and promote resilience in the aftermath of a crisis:

1. Mobile Learning Solutions:
   Innovation: Utilize mobile technology to deliver educational content, interactive lessons, and assessments.
   Benefits: Mobile learning is accessible, flexible, and can reach students in remote or displaced communities, overcoming infrastructure challenges.

2. Virtual and Augmented Reality (VR/AR):
   Innovation: Implement VR and AR technologies to create immersive learning experiences.
   Benefits: VR and AR can enhance engagement, provide virtual field trips, and simulate practical learning scenarios, compensating for disruptions in traditional education.

3. Online Tutoring Platforms:

Innovation: Establish online tutoring platforms connecting students with qualified tutors.

Benefits: Virtual tutoring provides personalized support, addresses learning gaps, and ensures continuity in education, especially in subjects requiring additional assistance.

4. Open Educational Resources (OER):

Innovation: Promote the use of freely accessible OER, including textbooks, videos, and interactive content.

Benefits: OER reduces educational costs, increases access to quality materials, and facilitates collaborative content creation and adaptation.

5. PeertoPeer Learning Networks:

Innovation: Facilitate peertopeer learning networks where students can collaborate and share knowledge.

Benefits: Peer learning promotes social interaction, encourages collaborative problem solving, and leverages the collective expertise of a community.

6. Community Learning Centers:

Innovation: Establish community learning centers that serve as hubs for education, providing resources, technology, and mentorship.

Benefits: Community centers offer a supportive learning environment, particularly for those without access to traditional school settings.

7. Gamified Learning Platforms:

Innovation: Integrate gamification elements into educational platforms to enhance engagement and motivation.

Benefits: Gamification makes learning enjoyable, encourages competition, and provides immediate feedback, fostering a positive learning experience.

8. Blockchain for Credentialing:

Innovation: Implement blockchain technology for secure and verifiable credentialing and certification.

Benefits: Blockchain ensures the integrity of educational credentials, making it easier for students to showcase their achievements and qualifications.

9. Remote STEM Labs:

Innovation: Create virtual laboratories for science, technology, engineering, and mathematics (STEM) subjects.

Benefits: Virtual labs allow students to conduct experiments, simulations, and handson activities, even when physical labs are inaccessible.

10. Adaptive Learning Systems:

Innovation: Deploy adaptive learning systems that personalize educational content based on individual student progress.

Benefits: Adaptive systems cater to diverse learning styles, pace, and abilities, ensuring that each student receives tailored support.

11. Microlearning Modules:

Innovation: Develop microlearning modules that deliver content in short, focused segments.

Benefits: Microlearning is easily digestible, accommodates varied attention spans, and allows for flexible scheduling, making it suitable for remote or disrupted learning environments.

12. Digital Literacy Programs:

Innovation: Integrate digital literacy programs into the curriculum to equip students with essential skills for online learning.

Benefits: Digital literacy empowers students to navigate online platforms, critically evaluate information, and utilize technology effectively.

13. Interactive Storytelling Platforms:

Innovation: Create interactive storytelling platforms that combine narrative elements with educational content.

Benefits: Interactive storytelling enhances engagement,

fosters creativity, and allows students to participate actively in the learning process.

14. Teacher Professional Development Platforms:
Innovation: Develop online platforms for teacher professional development, including training in remote teaching methods.
Benefits: Continuous professional development ensures that educators are equipped with the skills needed for effective online and blended learning.

15. Global Collaborative Projects:
Innovation: Facilitate global collaborative projects that connect students across borders to work on shared initiatives.
Benefits: Collaborative projects promote cultural exchange, global awareness, and the development of skills for working in diverse environments.

These innovative approaches leverage technology, community engagement, and creative pedagogies to address education gaps and provide inclusive learning opportunities, particularly in the challenging aftermath of a crisis. By embracing such innovations, education systems can become more resilient and better equipped to adapt to changing circumstances while ensuring access to quality education for all.

Technology plays a transformative role in shaping the future of education, influencing how students learn, teachers instruct, and educational institutions operate. The integration of technology in education has the potential to enhance accessibility, flexibility, and the overall quality of learning experiences. Here are key aspects of the role of technology in shaping the future of education:

1. Access to Education:
Role: Technology can bridge geographical and socioeconomic gaps, providing access to education for individuals in remote or underserved areas.
Impact: Online courses, digital resources, and elearning

platforms make education more accessible to diverse populations breaking down traditional barriers.

2. Personalized Learning:

Role: Technology enables adaptive learning platforms and personalized educational content tailored to individual student needs.

Impact: Personalized learning caters to different learning styles and paces, promoting student engagement and a deeper understanding of subjects.

3. Blended Learning Environments:

Role: Blending traditional classroom instruction with online components.

Impact: Blended learning allows for a flexible and interactive learning experience, combining face-to-face interactions with the advantages of digital resources.

4. Digital Collaboration and Communication:

Role: Technology facilitates collaboration among students and educators regardless of geographical locations.

Impact: Digital communication tools, collaborative platforms, and virtual classrooms enhance teamwork, communication, and information sharing.

5. Virtual Reality (VR) and Augmented Reality (AR):

Role: Immersive technologies like VR and AR create interactive and engaging learning experiences.

Impact: Virtual field trips, simulations, and interactive 3D models enhance understanding and provide hands on experiences, especially in subjects like science and geography.

6. Artificial Intelligence (AI) in Education:

Role: AI is used for adaptive learning, automated grading, and personalized recommendations.

Impact: AI analyzes student performance data, identifies learning patterns, and offers tailored suggestions, improving learning outcomes and efficiency.

7. Gamification of Learning:

Role: Applying game elements to educational content.

Impact: Gamification increases student engagement, motivation, and participation by incorporating elements like competition, rewards, and storytelling into the learning experience.

8. Online Assessment and Feedback:

Role: Utilizing digital tools for assessments and providing immediate feedback.

Impact: Online assessments streamline grading, allow for timely feedback, and enable data driven insights into student progress.

9. Ebooks and Open Educational Resources (OER):

Role: Digital textbooks and freely accessible educational resources.

Impact: Ebooks and OER reduce costs, ensure up-to-date content, and enhance accessibility, making educational materials widely available.

10. Blockchain for Credentialing:

Role: Blockchain technology provides secure and verifiable credentialing.

Impact: Blockchain ensures the integrity of academic credentials, making it easier for individuals to share and verify their educational achievements.

11. Data Analytics in Education:

Role: Analyzing data to gain insights into student performance, engagement, and learning patterns.

Impact: Data analytics helps educators make informed decisions, identify areas for improvement, and personalize learning experiences.

12. Flipped Classroom Model:

Role: Shifting traditional lecture based instruction to online learning outside the classroom, with in person sessions for collaborative activities.

Impact: The flipped classroom model maximizes class time for interactive discussions, problem solving and hands-on activities.

13. Remote and Online Learning Platforms:

Role: Online platforms provide opportunities for remote learning and distance education.

Impact: Especially crucial during crises, remote learning platforms allow for continued education, offering flexibility and accessibility.

14. Teacher Professional Development:

Role: Technology supports ongoing professional development for educators.

Impact: Online courses, webinars, and collaborative platforms empower teachers to enhance their skills, stay updated on best practices, and connect with a global community of educators.

15. Internet of Things (IoT) in Education:

Role: IoT devices enhance connectivity and data collection in educational settings.

Impact: Smart classrooms, wearable devices, and connected educational tools contribute to a more interactive and data rich learning environment.

The integration of technology in education is a dynamic process that continually evolves to meet the changing needs of students and educators. While offering numerous benefits, it is essential to address challenges such as the digital divide, privacy concerns, and the need for adequate training. The future of education is likely to see further advancements in technology, emphasizing inclusivity, adaptability and the enhancement of learning experiences for all.

CHAPTER IX

Building Resilient Societies

The need for long-term infrastructure and healthcare system planning is crucial for ensuring the sustainability, resilience, and effectiveness of healthcare services. This planning encompasses a wide range of considerations, from physical infrastructure to the organization and delivery of healthcare services. Here are key reasons highlighting the importance of long-term planning in both infrastructure and healthcare systems:

1. Population Growth and Aging:

Challenge: Growing populations and aging demographics place increased demands on healthcare services.

Need for Planning: Long-term planning is essential to anticipate and accommodate the healthcare needs of a larger and older population, including the development of adequate healthcare infrastructure and services.

2. Public Health Emergencies and Pandemics:

Challenge: Public health emergencies, such as pandemics, can strain healthcare systems to their limits.

Need for Planning: Long-term planning involves establishing robust emergency response mechanisms, ensuring adequate healthcare facilities, and developing surge capacity to handle unexpected crises.

3. Advancements in Medical Technology:

Challenge: Rapid advancements in medical technology require ongoing adaptation and integration into healthcare systems.

Need for Planning: Long-term planning involves adopting and incorporating new technologies, ensuring that healthcare infrastructure can support and leverage innovations to improve patient care.

4. Infrastructure Resilience and Sustainability:

Challenge: Aging infrastructure and vulnerability to natural disasters can disrupt healthcare services.

Need for Planning: Long-term planning includes investing in resilient and sustainable healthcare infrastructure to withstand shocks, minimize disruptions, and ensure continuous service delivery.

5. Chronic Disease Burden:

Challenge: Increasing prevalence of chronic diseases requires ongoing healthcare management and support.

Need for Planning: Long-term planning involves designing healthcare systems that can effectively manage and prevent chronic diseases, including the development of preventive care programs and patient centered services.

6. Access to Healthcare Services:

Challenge: Disparities in healthcare access and distribution can lead to unequal health outcomes.

Need for Planning: Long-term planning aims to address healthcare disparities by strategically locating healthcare facilities, improving transportation infrastructure, and implementing telehealth solutions to enhance accessibility.

7. Workforce Planning:

Challenge: Healthcare workforce shortages and maldistribution can impact the delivery of care.

Need for Planning: Long-term planning involves forecasting workforce needs, implementing training and education programs, and adopting policies to attract and retain healthcare professionals.

8. Financial Sustainability:

Challenge: Rising healthcare costs can strain financial resources.

Need for Planning: Long-term planning includes implementing cost-effective measures, exploring alternative funding models, and ensuring financial sustainability to maintain quality healthcare services.

9. Health Information Systems:

Challenge: Inefficient health information systems can hinder communication and coordination.

Need for Planning: Long-term planning involves the implementation of robust health information systems, including electronic health records, to enhance data sharing, communication, and decision making.

10. Community and Primary Care Integration:

Challenge: Gaps in community and primary care can lead to unmet health needs.

Need for Planning: Long-term planning includes integrating community and primary care services, promoting preventive care, and establishing networks to address the broader health needs of communities.

11. Global Health Threats:

Challenge: Global health threats, such as infectious diseases, require coordinated international responses.

Need for Planning: Long-term planning involves collaboration at the global level, sharing resources, and developing strategies to address and mitigate the impact of global health threats.

12. Telehealth and Digital Health Integration:

Challenge: Limited integration of telehealth and digital health solutions.

Need for Planning: Long-term planning involves incorporating telehealth and digital health into healthcare systems, ensuring widespread access, and leveraging technology to improve patient outcomes and streamline healthcare delivery.

13. Preparedness for Emerging Health Issues:

Challenge: Emerging health issues, such as new infectious

diseases or health crises, require proactive preparedness.

Need for Planning: Long-term planning involves establishing frameworks for rapid response, research, and coordination to address emerging health threats effectively.

14. Regulatory and Policy Adaptation:

Challenge: Rapid changes in healthcare regulations and policies can impact service delivery.

Need for Planning: Long-term planning includes adaptability to evolving regulations, policy frameworks, and the development of agile systems that can respond to changing healthcare landscapes.

15. Patient Centered Care:

Challenge: Ensuring that healthcare services are patient centered requires intentional design and organizational changes.

Need for Planning: Long-term planning focuses on creating patient centric healthcare systems that prioritize individual needs, preferences, and experiences.

In summary, Long-term infrastructure and healthcare system planning are essential for addressing current challenges, preparing for future uncertainties, and ensuring the delivery of high quality, accessible, and sustainable healthcare services. Strategic planning allows healthcare systems to adapt to evolving needs, leverage technological advancements, and enhance the overall health and well-being of populations.

Mitigating environmental impact and addressing resource scarcity are critical challenges that require comprehensive strategies at individual, community, corporate, and governmental levels. Here are strategies for mitigating environmental impact and promoting sustainable resource use:

1. Renewable Energy Transition:

Strategy: Transitioning from fossil fuels to renewable energy sources (solar, wind, hydropower).

Impact: Reduces greenhouses gas emissions, decrease reliance on finite resources, and promote a cleaner energy future.

2. Energy Efficiency Measures:

Strategy: Implementing energy efficient technologies and practices.

Impact: Reduces overall energy consumption, lowers environmental impact, and contributes to resource conservation.

3. Circular Economy Practices:

Strategy: Adopting circular economy principles to minimize waste and promote recycling.

Impact: Enhances resource efficiency, reduces landfill waste, and promotes the reuse and recycling of materials.

4. Sustainable Agriculture:

Strategy: Implementing sustainable farming practices and reducing reliance on chemical inputs.

Impact: Preserves soil health, reduces water usage, minimizes chemical runoff, and promotes biodiversity.

5. Water Conservation:

Strategy: Implementing water saving technologies and promoting water conservation practices.

Impact: Addresses water scarcity, reduces the environmental impact of water extraction, and ensures sustainable water use.

6. Waste Reduction and Management:

Strategy: Implementing waste reduction measures and improving waste management systems.

Impact: Minimizes landfills waste, encourages recycling, and reduces pollution.

7. Biodiversity Conservation:

Strategy: Implementing conservation measures to protect and restore biodiversity.

Impact: Preserves ecosystems, supports natural pollinators, and contributes to overall environmental health.

8. Green Building and Infrastructure:

Strategy: Constructing energy efficient and environmentally friendly buildings and infrastructure.

Impact: Reduces energy consumption, minimizes environmental footprint, and promotes sustainable urban development.

9. Sustainable Transportation:

Strategy: Promoting public transportation, electric vehicles, and alternative transportation modes.

Impact: Reduces emissions, decreases reliance on fossil fuels, and addresses air quality issues.

10. Responsible Consumption and Production:

Strategy: Promoting sustainable and ethical consumption patterns.

Impact: Reduces demand for environmentally harmful products, encourages responsible production practices, and minimizes waste.

11. Corporate Social Responsibility (CSR):

Strategy: Integrating sustainability into corporate practices and supply chains.

Impact: Encourages responsible business practices, reduces environmental impact, and fosters transparency and accountability.

12. Government Policies and Regulations:

Strategy: Implementing and enforcing environmental regulations and policies.

Impact: Sets standards for sustainable practices, incentivizes green initiatives, and ensures compliance with environmental laws. All must be consistent with human prosperity and reasoned logical considerations.

13. Education and Awareness Programs:

Strategy: Promoting environmental education and awareness.

Impact: Empowers individuals to make sustainable choices, encourage ecofriendly behaviors, and fosters a culture of environmental stewardship.

14. Collaboration and Partnerships:
Strategy: Encouraging collaboration between governments, businesses, NGOs, and communities.
Impact: Facilitates the sharing of resources, knowledge, and expertise to address environmental challenges collectively.

15. Investment in Green Technologies:
Strategy: Supporting research and development of green technologies.
Impact: Drives innovation, accelerates the adoption of sustainable practices, and contributes to the development of ecofriendly solutions. However, not to the determent of current practices until such time as they can be effectively and appropriately replaced.

16. Natural Resource Management:
Strategy: Implementing sustainable practices in resource extraction and management.
Impact: Preserves ecosystems, prevents resource depletion, and supports the responsible use of natural resources.

17. Carbon Offset Programs:
Strategy: Investing in projects that reasonably offset carbon emissions.
Impact: Compensates for carbon emissions, promotes sustainable projects, and implement further climate change investigations into verifiable carbon damage to the environment.

18. Sustainable Fisheries Practices:
Strategy: Implementing responsible fishing practices and protecting marine ecosystems.
Impact: Preserves fish stocks, supports marine biodiversity, and ensures the Long-term sustainability of fisheries.

19. Incentives for Green Innovation:
Strategy: Offering financial incentives and rewards for

businesses and individuals adopting sustainable practices.

Impact: Encourages the development and adoption of ecofriendly technologies and practices.

20. Community Engagement and Empowerment:

Strategy: Engaging communities in environmental initiatives and empowering them to take active roles.

Impact: Builds a sense of environmental responsibility, fosters local sustainability efforts, and strengthens community resilience.

Mitigating environmental impact and addressing resource scarcity require a holistic and integrated approach. By implementing these strategies, stakeholders can contribute to a more sustainable and resilient future, promoting the well being of both the planet and its inhabitants.

Urban planning plays a crucial role in building resilient communities, especially in the face of challenges such as climate change, natural disasters, population growth, and social and economic uncertainties. Resilient communities are those that can effectively anticipate, respond to, recover from, and adapt to shocks and stresses. Here's an examination of the key aspects of the role of urban planning in building resilient communities:

1. Risk Assessment and Mitigation:

Urban Planning Role: Conducting risk assessments to identify vulnerabilities and potential hazards.

Impact: Urban planning helps develop strategies to mitigate risks, such as avoiding construction in flood prone areas or implementing building codes to withstand earthquakes.

2. Land Use Planning:

Urban Planning Role: Determining how land is used and zoning regulations.

Impact: Proper land use planning can minimize exposure to environmental risks and ensure those essential services and infrastructure is strategically located to serve the community efficiently.

3. Infrastructure Resilience:

Urban Planning Role: Designing and implementing resilient infrastructure systems.

Impact: Robust infrastructure, including transportation, water supply, and energy systems, enhances the community's ability to withstand and recover from shocks and disruptions.

4. Green Spaces and Urban Design:

Urban Planning Role: Incorporating green spaces and sustainable urban design.

Impact: Green infrastructure improves environmental quality, provides natural buffers against disasters, and enhances community well being.

5. Community Engagement:

Urban Planning Role: Facilitating community participation in the planning process.

Impact: Engaging residents ensures that planning decisions reflect local needs, values, and knowledge, fostering a sense of ownership and community cohesion.

6. Affordable Housing and Social Equity:

Urban Planning Role: Addressing housing affordability and promoting social equity.

Impact: Ensuring that housing is affordable and accessible to diverse income groups contributes to social resilience by preventing displacement during crises.

7. MultiModal Transportation:

Urban Planning Role: Developing integrated and multimodal transportation systems.

Impact: Diverse and efficient transportation options enhance community resilience by providing alternatives during disruptions and reducing dependence on a single mode of transportation.

8. Climate Responsive Planning:
   Urban Planning Role: Integrating climate responsive strategies into planning processes.
   Impact: Adaptation measures, such as flood resistant infrastructure and climate resilient building codes, help communities withstand the impacts of weather effects.

9. Economic Diversification:
   Urban Planning Role: Encouraging economic diversification and local resilience.
   Impact: A diverse local economy is more adaptable to economic shocks, reducing vulnerability to disruptions in specific sectors.

10. Emergency Preparedness and Response:
   Urban Planning Role: Developing emergency preparedness and response plans.
   Impact: Planning for emergencies, including evacuation routes, shelters, and communication strategies, enhances community resilience in the face of natural disasters or other crises.

11. Smart City Technologies:
   Urban Planning Role: Integrating smart technologies for data driven decision-making.
   Impact: Smart city technologies enhance situational awareness, improve response times, and optimize resource allocation during emergencies.

12. Crisis Communication Systems:
   Urban Planning Role: Establishing effective communication systems.
   Impact: Communication infrastructure ensures that timely and accurate information reaches the community during emergencies, helping residents' make-informed decisions.

13. Social Infrastructure Planning:
   Urban Planning Role: Planning for social infrastructure,

including healthcare and educational facilities.

Impact: Adequate social infrastructure supports community well being and ensures that essential services are available during and after crises.

14. Regenerative Urban Design:

Urban Planning Role: Embracing regenerative design principles.

Impact: Regenerative urban design goes beyond sustainability, aiming to restore and enhance ecosystems, fostering resilience against environmental degradation.

15. Resilient Urban Policies:

Urban Planning Role: Formulating policies that promote resilience.

Impact: Legal and policy frameworks support the implementation of resilient measures and ensure that planning decisions align with Long-term community goals.

16. Community Capacity Building:

Urban Planning Role: Supporting community capacity building initiatives.

Impact: Strengthening local skills, knowledge, and resources empowers communities to actively contribute to their own resilience.

17. Adaptive Reuse of Spaces:

Urban Planning Role: Encouraging the adaptive reuse of spaces.

Impact: Adaptive reuse supports the revitalization of existing structures, reducing the need for new construction and promoting sustainability.

18. Monitoring and Evaluation:

Urban Planning Role: Establishing monitoring and evaluation mechanisms.

Impact: Regular assessment and feedback loops allow for the refinement of plans, ensuring their effectiveness in enhancing community resilience.

19. Cross-Sectional Collaboration:
Urban Planning Role: Facilitating collaboration across sectors and disciplines.
Impact: Collaboration ensures a holistic approach to resilience, leveraging expertise from various fields to address complex challenges.

20. Learning from Past Events:
Urban Planning Role: Analyzing and learning from past events.
Impact: Understanding the lessons from previous crises informs future-planning efforts, improving the community's ability to anticipate and respond to challenges.

By integrating these strategies, urban planning contributes to the creation of resilient communities capable of adapting and thriving in the face of diverse challenges, fostering sustainability, well being, and a high quality of life for residents.

CHAPTER X

Towards a New Normal

The global workforce has experienced significant shifts in work culture, with the prevalence of remote work being a key transformation. Several factors, including technological advancements, changes in employee preferences, and the impact of the COVID19 pandemic, have accelerated the adoption of remote work. Here's a discussion of the shifts in work culture and the prevalence of remote work:

1. Technological Advancements:
   Shift: The evolution of digital technologies, highspeed internet, cloud computing, and collaboration tools has enabled seamless remote work.
   Impact: Employees can connect and collaborate from anywhere, reducing the dependence on physical office spaces.

2. Flexibility and Work Life Balance:
   Shift: There is a growing emphasis on flexibility and work life balance.
   Impact: Remote work allows employees to create customized work schedules, contributing to improved work life balance and job satisfaction.

3. Remote Work during the COVID19 Pandemic:
   Shift: The pandemic necessitated a widespread shift to remote work.
   Impact: Organizations adapted to remote work as a safety measure, and many continued to embrace it due to its success in maintaining productivity.

4. Hybrid Work Models:

Shift: Many organizations are adopting hybrid work models that combine remote and in office work.

Impact: Hybrid models offer flexibility while maintaining some level of in person collaboration, catering to diverse employee preferences.

5. Digital Collaboration Tools:

Shift: The proliferation of digital collaboration tools (e.g., video conferencing, project management platforms) has facilitated remote communication.

Impact: Teams can collaborate effectively, conduct virtual meetings, and manage projects in realtime, regardless of physical location.

6. Focus on Results and Output:

Shift: A shift from traditional timebased assessment to outcome based evaluation.

Impact: Remote work encourages a results oriented approach, emphasizing the quality and impact of work over hours spent in the office.

7. Global Talent Pool:

Shift: Remote work allows organizations to tap into a global talent pool.

Impact: Companies can access diverse skill sets and perspectives, fostering innovation and increasing competitiveness.

8. Emphasis on Employee Well-being:

Shift: Organizations are increasingly prioritizing employee well-being.

Impact: Remote work can contribute to reduced stress and better mental health by providing employees with a more flexible and comfortable work environment.

9. Changes in Communication Dynamics:

Shift: Communication dynamics have evolved with increased reliance on digital communication.

Impact: Remote work emphasizes asynchronous communication, and organizations need to adapt to different modes of interaction.

10. Adoption of Remote On boarding and Training:
Shift: Remote work has necessitated the adoption of virtual on boarding and training programs.
Impact: Companies are leveraging technology to onboard and train employees remotely, ensuring a smooth transition and continuous development.

11. Impact on Commercial Real Estate:
Shift: Reduced dependence on physical office spaces.
Impact: Organizations reconsider their real estate needs, potentially leading to changes in office space requirements and locations.

12. Challenges of Remote Work:
Shift: Recognition of challenges associated with remote work, such as potential isolation and blurred work life boundaries.
Impact: Organizations are actively addressing these challenges through policies, support mechanisms, and employee engagement initiatives.

13. Digital Security Concerns:
Shift: Increased reliance on digital tools raises cybersecurity concerns.
Impact: Organizations are investing in robust cybersecurity measures to protect sensitive information and maintain data security in a remote work environment.

14. Shift in Leadership Styles:
Shift: Remote work has influenced leadership styles towards increased trust and empowerment.
Impact: Leaders are focusing on outcomes, fostering trust, and providing support to remote teams.

15. Reevaluation of Business Continuity Plans:

Shift: The pandemic highlighted the importance of robust business continuity plans.

Impact: Organizations are reassessing and strengthening their continuity plans to ensure resilience in the face of future disruptions.

16. Emphasis on Employee Experience:

Shift: A growing emphasis on enhancing the overall employee experience.

Impact: Organizations are investing in tools, policies, and initiatives that contribute to a positive and inclusive remote work experience.

17. Government and Regulatory Considerations:

Shift: Governments and regulatory bodies are adapting to the remote work trend.

Impact: Policies and regulations related to remote work are evolving, addressing legal, tax, and compliance considerations.

18. Shift in Employee Expectations:

Shift: Employees now expect greater flexibility in work arrangements.

Impact: Organizations need to align their policies with employee expectations to attract and retain top talent.

19. Investment in Employee Engagement Initiatives:

Shift: Increased investment in employee engagement initiatives for remote teams.

Impact: Organizations are implementing virtual teambuilding activities, wellness programs, and recognition initiatives to foster a sense of connection and belonging.

20. Learning and Development Opportunities:

Shift: Remote work has prompted a shift in how organizations deliver learning and development opportunities.

Impact: Virtual training programs, webinars, and online resources are increasingly being utilized to support professional growth in a remote work environment.

The prevalence of remote work represents a transformative shift in the way people work, and it has implications for organizational culture, employee well-being, and business operations. As organizations continue to adapt to these changes, a flexible and adaptive approach to work culture will be essential for building resilience and sustaining productivity in the evolving landscape of work.

The dynamics of urban and rural life have been undergoing significant changes influenced by factors such as demographic shifts, technological advancements, economic transformations, and societal preferences. These changes contribute to the evolving landscapes of both urban and rural areas, impacting lifestyle, infrastructure, and community dynamics. Here is an exploration of the changing dynamics of urban and rural life:

Changing Dynamics of Urban Life:

1. Population Growth and Urbanization:
   Change: Rapid population growth and urbanization.
   Impact: Cities are experiencing increased density, leading to challenges in housing, infrastructure, and public services.

2. Technological Advancements:
   Change: Integration of advanced technologies in urban environments.
   Impact: Smart cities are emerging, incorporating technologies for efficient transportation, energy management, and public services.

3. Shift in Housing Preferences:
   Change: Changing preferences towards urban living.
   Impact: Increased demand for mixed use developments, walkable neighborhoods, and proximity to amenities.

4. Remote Work and Flexible Work Arrangements:
   Change: Rise in remote work and flexible work arrangements.
   Impact: Urban residents have greater flexibility to choose

living locations, potentially leading to shifts in city demographics.

5. Cultural and Entertainment Hubs:
   Change: Urban areas as cultural and entertainment hubs.
   Impact: Cities attract residents and visitors with diverse cultural events, entertainment options, and nightlife.

6. Transportation Trends:
   Change: Evolution of transportation modes and increased focus on sustainability.
   Impact: Growth in public transportation, bike sharing, and walking infrastructure, alongside a move towards electric and autonomous vehicles.

7. Gentrification and Housing Affordability:
   Change: Gentrification leading to changes in neighborhood demographics.
   Impact: Rising property values may lead to displacement, affecting housing affordability and community composition.

8. Focus on Sustainability:
   Change: Growing emphasis on sustainable urban development.
   Impact: Implementation of green infrastructure, renewable energy initiatives, and ecofriendly urban planning.

9. Social and Cultural Diversity:
   Change: Urban areas as melting pots of diversity.
   Impact: Increased exposure to diverse cultures, ideas, and lifestyles, contributing to cultural richness and tolerance.

10. Amenities and Services Accessibility:
   Change: Improved accessibility to amenities and services.
   Impact: Cities offer a wide range of services, healthcare facilities, educational institutions, and recreational opportunities.

Changing Dynamics of Rural Life:

1. Population Decline in Some Rural Areas:

Change: Population decline in certain rural regions.

Impact: Challenges in maintaining local services, infrastructure, and sustaining community vitality.

2. Technological Connectivity:

Change: Advancements in rural connectivity.

Impact: Improved internet access and communication technologies, enabling remote work, online education, and telehealth services.

3. Agricultural Transformations:

Change: Technological advancements in agriculture.

Impact: Increased efficiency, automation, and precision agriculture practices, transforming the rural economy.

4. Tourism and Rural Development:

Change: Growing interest in rural tourism.

Impact: Rural areas attract tourists seeking natural landscapes, outdoor activities, and unique cultural experiences.

5. Remote Work Opportunities:

Change: Remote work opportunities influencing rural living choices.

Impact: Individuals and families may choose rural areas for a higher quality of life, affordability, and natural surroundings.

6. Renewable Energy Projects:

Change: Implementation of renewable energy projects in rural areas.

Impact: Rural regions may become hubs for wind, solar, or biomass energy production, contributing to sustainability.

7. Local Food Movements:

Change: Rise in demand for locally produced food.

Impact: Support for local agriculture, farmers' markets, and community supported agriculture (CSA) initiatives.

8. Community Led Initiatives:

Change: Growth in community led initiatives.

Impact: Residents actively participate in local decision making, sustainable development, and community projects.

9. Education and Healthcare Access:
   Change: Challenges in accessing education and healthcare.
   Impact: Efforts to improve rural education and healthcare services to address disparities.

10. Preservation of Natural Landscapes:
   Change: Focus on preserving rural landscapes and biodiversity.
   Impact: Conservation efforts to protect natural resources, wildlife habitats, and promote ecotourism.

Overarching Trends:

1. Blurring Boundaries:
   Trend: Blurring distinctions between urban and rural.
   Impact: Increased connectivity allows for a more fluid lifestyle, with individuals and families blending urban amenities with rural tranquility.

2. Economic Diversification:
   Trend: Economic diversification in both urban and rural areas.
   Impact: A shift from traditional economic activities, with a growing emphasis on technology, services, and innovation.

3. Environmental Awareness:
   Trend: Growing environmental awareness in both settings.
   Impact: Sustainability practices become integral to both urban and rural development, promoting ecofriendly initiatives.

4. Community Resilience:
   Trend: Emphasis on building community resilience.
   Impact: Communities, whether urban or rural, focus on collaborative efforts, social cohesion, and preparedness for challenges.

5. Individualized Choices:

Trend: Increasing emphasis on individual lifestyle choices.

Impact: Individuals have the flexibility to choose living environments that align with their values, preferences, and work arrangements.

6. Technology as an Equalizer:

Trend: Technology bridging gaps between urban and rural areas.

Impact: Access to digital tools, education, healthcare, and economic opportunities become more equitable.

7. Policy Interventions:

Trend: Government policies addressing urban and rural disparities.

Impact: Interventions to support infrastructure development, economic growth, and quality of life enhancements in both settings.

8. Resilient Local Economies:

Trend: Promotion of resilient local economies.

Impact: Encouragement of diverse economic activities that enhance local self-sufficiency and reduce dependence on external factors.

The changing dynamics of urban and rural life reflect the complexities of modern society, with a focus on sustainable, inclusive, and technologically enabled communities. As individuals, communities, and policymakers navigate these changes, the goal is often to create environments that offer a high quality of life, economic opportunities, and environmental stewardship.

Vision for a Resilient and Adaptive Future: "Sustainable Horizons 2035"

In the year 2035, we envision a world that has embraced resilience and adaptability as core principles, fostering a harmonious coexistence between humanity and the planet. "Sustainable

Horizons 2035" represents a future where communities, ecosystems, and economies thrive in the face of challenges, equipped with the tools, mindset, and infrastructure to navigate an ever-changing world. This vision encompasses key pillars that define our path towards a resilient and adaptive future:

1. Holistic Well-being:
A society that prioritizes the well being of individuals and communities.

Integrated healthcare systems focusing on preventive care, mental health, and community support.

Education systems nurturing holistic development, critical thinking, and adaptability.

2. EcoCentric Urbanism and Rural Harmony:
Sustainable, green cities designed for both ecological health and human well being.

Regenerative rural landscapes promoting biodiversity, local food production, and community led initiatives.

Blurred boundaries between urban and rural, fostering a balance between nature and technology.

3. Digital Inclusion and Connectivity:
Universal access to digital technologies for education, work, and healthcare.

Equitable and affordable highspeed internet connecting urban and rural areas.

Digital literacy programs empowering all members of society.

4. Climate Resilience and Circular Economies:
Robust strategies to mitigate and adapt to climate change impacts.

Circular economies minimizing waste, promoting recycling, and sustainable resource use.

Green infrastructure and sustainable practices integrated into urban planning and industry.

5. Inclusive Economies and Social Equity:

Inclusive economic models reducing income disparities and fostering social equity.

Local and global partnerships supporting fair trade, ethical business practices, and community driven initiatives.

Social safety nets ensuring resilience against economic shocks.

6. Renewable Energy and Technological Innovation:
Reasonable transition to renewable energy sources for a sustainable future.

Innovation hubs driving sustainable technologies, from green energy solutions to ecofriendly transportation.

Ethical AI and technology to enhance human potential while preserving privacy and ethical standards.

7. Community Empowerment and Governance:
Decentralized governance structures empowering local communities.

Collaborative decision making processes incorporating diverse voices and perspectives.

Civic engagement and participatory approaches in shaping policies and initiatives.

8. Global Cooperation and Peaceful Coexistence:
Strengthened international collaborations to address global challenges.

Diplomacy and dialogue as primary tools for conflict resolution and global governance.

Collective efforts for peace, humanitarian aid, and sustainable development worldwide.

9. Resilient Food Systems and Water Security:
Sustainable agriculture practices ensuring food security and minimizing environmental impact.

Water management strategies addressing scarcity, pollution, and equitable distribution.

Locally sourced, diverse diets supporting health and sustainable food systems.

10. Education for Lifelong Learning:

Education systems emphasizing lifelong learning, adaptability, and critical thinking.

Integration of technology in education to enhance accessibility and personalized learning.

Emphasis on creativity, emotional intelligence, and interdisciplinary skills.

11. Cultural Diversity and Inclusivity:

Celebration and preservation of cultural diversity as a source of strength.

Inclusive cultural narratives promoting understanding, tolerance, and unity.

Support for indigenous knowledge, languages, and heritage.

12. Nature Based Solutions and Conservation:

Adoption of nature based solutions to address environmental challenges.

Protected natural spaces, reforestation projects, and conservation efforts.

Coexistence with nature as a fundamental principle guiding human activities.

"Sustainable Horizons 2035" represents a collective commitment to building a resilient and adaptive future that honors the interconnectedness of humanity and the planet. It is a vision where individuals, communities, and nations work together, drawing inspiration from the lessons of the past and guided by a shared responsibility for the well being of future generations. In this future, the pursuit of sustainability, adaptability, and resilience becomes a journey that transcends borders, enriching the tapestry of human existence on Earth.

CONCLUSION

In this extensive conversation, we've delved into a wide array of topics spanning from essential human survival needs to envisioning a resilient and adaptive future. Here's a holistic conclusion summarizing the key insights and discussions:

1. Human Survival Essentials:

Explored the four fundamental elements crucial for human survival: air, water, food, and shelter.

Emphasized the significance of air and the need for clean, breathable air for sustaining life.

Discussed strategies for securing these essentials, including sustainable practices and resource management.

2. Post crisis Prosperity Topics:

Identified 50 topics likely to be in demand for post crisis prosperity, covering diverse areas such as healthcare, technology, sustainable living, and global cooperation.

Recognized the importance of adaptability and innovation in shaping a prosperous future.

3. Resilience and Adaptation:

Explored the changing dynamics of urban and rural life, acknowledging the impact of technological advancements, demographic shifts, and societal preferences.

Discussed the role of urban planning in building resilient communities, emphasizing holistic approaches to infrastructure, community engagement, and sustainability.

4. Remote Work and Work Culture Shifts:

Examined the shifts in work culture, driven by technological advancements, remote work trends, and changing expectations.

Explored the challenges and opportunities presented by

remote work, including its impact on work life balance, communication dynamics, and the future of the traditional office.

5. Global Resilience and Environmental Sustainability:

Explored strategies for mitigating environmental impact and resource scarcity, recognizing the importance of renewable energy, circular economies, and responsible consumption.

Discussed the role of urban planning in building resilient communities and promoting sustainability.

6. Changing Dynamics of Urban and Rural Life:

Highlighted the evolving landscapes of urban and rural areas, influenced by factors such as technology, demographics, and economic transformations.

Recognized the importance of building resilient, inclusive, and technologically enabled communities in both urban and rural settings.

7. Envisioning a Resilient Future:

Proposed a vision for the future, "Sustainable Horizons 2035," emphasizing holistic well being, ecocentric urbanism, digital inclusion, and global cooperation.

Envisioned a future where resilience, adaptability, and sustainability are central principles guiding societal, economic, and environmental development.

In conclusion, our discussions have navigated through the essentials of human survival, the challenges and opportunities presented by crises, the transformations in work culture, the dynamics of urban and rural life, and the vision for a resilient and adaptive future. The overarching theme underscores the importance of collective efforts, innovation, and a commitment to sustainability in shaping a prosperous and harmonious world for generations to come.

RECOMMENDATIONS

Here are practical recommendations for individuals, communities, and policymakers to contribute to a resilient and adaptive future:

For Individuals:

1. Adopt Sustainable Practices:
    Embrace sustainable living habits, such as reducing single use plastic, conserving water, and minimizing energy consumption.

2. Stay Informed:
    Stay informed about local and global issues, including environmental concerns, public health, and community development.

3. Invest in Education:
    Prioritize continuous learning and skill development to enhance adaptability in a rapidly changing world.

4. Promote Inclusivity:
    Foster inclusivity and diversity in personal and professional networks, promoting understanding and tolerance.

5. Practice Mindful Consumption:
    Make conscious choices when consuming goods and services, supporting environmentally friendly and ethically produced products.

6. Engage in Community Initiatives:
    Participate in local community initiatives, volunteering, and collaborative projects to strengthen community bonds.

7. Advocate for Clean Transportation:
    Opt for ecofriendly transportation options, such as public

transit, cycling, carbon reduced emissions or electric vehicles.

8. Support Local Businesses:
Choose locally sourced products and support local businesses to contribute to the resilience of the local economy.

9. Invest in Health and Well-being:
Prioritize physical and mental health, adopting healthy lifestyle choices and seeking support when needed.

10. Embrace Digital Literacy:
Enhance digital literacy skills to adapt to evolving technologies and leverage digital tools for personal and professional growth.

For Communities:

1. Community Planning for Resilience:
Engage in community planning that prioritize resilience, considering factors like green spaces, emergency preparedness, and sustainable infrastructure.

2. Promote Local Initiatives:
Support and promote local initiatives, cooperatives, and community driven projects that enhance self-sufficiency.

3. Facilitate Inclusivity:
Create inclusive spaces that celebrate diversity and provide equal opportunities for all community members.

4. Establish Green Spaces:
Develop and maintain green spaces, community gardens, and recreational areas to enhance the overall well being of residents.

5. Community Education Programs:
Implement educational programs within the community that focus on environmental awareness, health, and skill development.

6. Collaborate with Local Government:
Collaborate with local government authorities to address

community needs, advocate for sustainable policies, and ensure effective governance.

7. Foster Social Cohesion:

Foster social cohesion through events, cultural exchanges, and initiatives that bring community members together.

8. Prepare for Emergencies:

Develop and communicate community wide emergency response plans, ensuring residents are prepared for potential crises.

9. Encourage Local Economy:

Support local businesses and markets to strengthen the local economy and reduce dependence on external factors.

10. Invest in Renewable Energy:

Explore and invest in renewable energy sources at the community level, promoting sustainability and reducing environmental impact.

For Policymakers:

1. Enact Sustainable Policies:

Implement policies that prioritize sustainability, renewable energy, reduced emission and environmentally responsible practices.

2. Invest in Education Systems:

Allocate resources to education systems that focus on fostering critical thinking, adaptability, and digital literacy.

3. Strengthen Healthcare Infrastructure:

Invest in robust healthcare infrastructure, ensuring accessibility and preparedness for health crises.

4. Support Local Economies:

Implement policies that support local businesses, entrepreneurs, and sustainable economic development.

5. Promote Green Infrastructure:

Encourage urban planning that incorporates green infrastructure, renewable energy, and sustainable transportation.

6. Incentivizes Renewable Energy Adoption:

Provide incentives for businesses and individuals to adopt renewable energy sources, fostering a transition to a greener economy.

7. Foster Innovation Hubs:

Create innovation hubs and research centers that focus on sustainable technologies, green practices, and advancements in various fields.

8. Prioritize Inclusive Policies:

Develop and implement policies that prioritize inclusivity, diversity, and equal opportunities for all members of society. With a focus on best practice for society's well being.

9. Invest in Resilience Training:

Allocate resources for community resilience training, including emergency response and disaster preparedness programs.

10. Global Collaboration:

Engage in international collaborations and agreements to address global challenges, such as climate change and public health crises.

By implementing these practical recommendations at the individual, community, and policymaker levels, we can collectively contribute to building a resilient, adaptive, and sustainable future. The integration of these efforts across different scales is essential for creating positive and lasting change.

Call to Action

Embracing Resilience: A Catalyst for Positive Change

In the tapestry of life, resilience stands as a powerful thread that weaves through our experiences, shaping not just survival but propelling us towards positive transformation. It is the unwavering spirit that emerges from adversity, turning challenges into stepping stones for growth. As we stand at the threshold of an ever-revolving world, embracing resilience becomes not just a choice but a catalyst for profound and positive change.

The Power of Adaptability:
Resilience is not merely about bouncing back; it's the art of bouncing forward. It's the ability to adapt, learn, and evolve in the face of uncertainty. Think of a tree standing tall in a storm, its branches swaying but roots firmly grounded. Similarly, embracing resilience allows us to navigate the storms of life, emerging stronger and more flexible.

Transforming Challenges into Opportunities:
Every setback, every trial, holds within it the seed of opportunity. Resilience transforms challenges into platforms for innovation and growth. It's in the midst of difficulties that we discover our untapped potential, finding creative solutions and redefining what's possible.

Cultivating Inner Strength:
Resilience is an inner journey, a cultivation of inner strength that transcends circumstances. It's the unwavering belief that, no matter the challenge, there's a reservoir of strength within to face it. This strength not only sustains us through hardships but becomes a beacon inspiring others on their journeys.

Building Bridges in Communities:
Communities that embrace resilience are the bedrock of positive change. In times of crisis, resilient communities come together, fostering a spirit of solidarity and mutual support. This shared resilience becomes a catalyst for community driven initiatives, creating positive ripples that extend far beyond individual efforts.

Fostering a Mindset of Possibility:
Resilience is a mindset that sees possibilities where others see barriers. It's a refusal to be defined by setbacks but rather to define them as moments of growth. This mindset of possibility is contagious, inspiring others to believe in their capacity to overcome challenges.

Embracing Change as a Constant:
In a world where change is the only constant, resilience is our compass. It's the guiding force that allows us not just to weather change but to embrace it as an opportunity for renewal. Resilience empowers us to let go of what no longer serves, opening the door to new beginnings.

Writing Our Stories of Triumph:
Each of us is the author of our story, and resilience is the ink that writes tales of triumph. It's not the absence of challenges that defines our narrative but our response to them. Embracing resilience allows us to write stories that inspire not just ourselves but those who come after, creating a legacy of strength.

A Call to Action:
Now, more than ever, the call to embrace resilience resonates loudly. It is a call to turn uncertainties into possibilities, setbacks into comebacks, and challenges into catalysts for positive change. As individuals, communities, and global citizens, let us become ambassadors of resilience, standing united in the face of adversity, and transforming the narrative of our shared future.

In the embrace of resilience, we find not just survival but the essence of what it means to truly thrive. It is a catalyst that propels us towards a future where challenges are not roadblocks but stepping stones, and each trial becomes an opportunity to manifest the incredible strength that resides within us. Together, let us embark on a journey of resilience, turning the page towards a future where positive change is not just a possibility but a promise waiting to be fulfilled.

ABOUT THE AUTHOR

Tl Bell

As a proponent of lifetime learning I endeavor to instill the same desire for knowledge in others. Knowledge is key in so many aspects of life. From making good decisions to taking actions that count. I created this series of guides as thought  provoking instruments for everyone to use for personal enrichment, prosperity and securing peace of mind.

BOOKS BY THIS AUTHOR

Understanding Communication: Pre And Post Crisis

Which Path? College Degree Or Entrepreneurship

Develop A Secondary Source Of Income: Strategy To Ensure Financial Stability During Economic Downturns

Wilderness Survival Skills: Learn How To Forage For Food, Find Clean Water, And Build Primitive Shelters

Understanding Communication: Pre And Post Crisis

Detecting And Countering Drones: Things To Consider

The Power Of Bartering: In A Post-Crisis World